Modern Critical Views

Modern Critical Views

JAMAICA KINCAID

Edited and with an introduction by
Harold Bloom
Sterling Professor of the Humanities
Yale University

CHELSEA HOUSE PUBLISHERS
Philadelphia

© 1998 by Chelsea House Publishers, a division of
Main Line Book Co.

Introduction © 1998 by Harold Bloom

Printed and bound in the United States of America

10 9 8 7 6 5 4 3 2

∞ The paper used in this publication meets the minimum
requirements of the American National Standard for
Permanence of Paper for Printed Library Materials,
Z39.48-1984

Library of Congress Cataloging-in-Publication Data

Jamaica Kincaid / edited and with an introduction by
  Harold Bloom.
        p. cm.—(Modern critical views)
    Includes bibliographical references and index.
    ISBN 0-7910-4781-4 (hc)
    1. Kincaid, Jamaica—Criticism and interpretation.
I. Bloom. Harold.   II. Series.
PR9275.A583K565   1998
813—dc21   98-14078
                                                                CIP

Contents

Editor's Note

This book presents a representative selection of the best criticism available upon the work of the Caribbean woman writer, Jamaica Kincaid. I am grateful to Tenley Williams for her skilled editorial assistance.

My Introduction meditates upon the question of Kincaid's characteristic genre, a blend of short story and prose poem, that I suggest is more traditional in literary mode than most of her critics assert.

The sequence of critical essays begins with Giovanna Covi's argument that Kincaid's particular strength is that her stories resist all canons. Laura Niesen de Abruna interestingly contrasts Kincaid with a "literary foremother," the Caribbean novelist Jean Rhys.

In Alison Donnell's view, Kincaid's *A Small Place* challenges postcolonial feminist critics to relocate many of their assumptions, while Moira Ferguson finds in *Lucy* "a new postcolonial cartography."

Patricia Ismond praises Kincaid for her renewal of the concept of childlike innocence, after which Susan Sniader Lanser discovers in Kincaid an invaluable resource for global feminism in its quest to free itself from what might be termed the stigma of "tourism."

Annie John is investigated by H. Adlai Murdoch as a highly successful achievement in cultural identity, while Edyta Oczkowicz returns us to *Lucy*, with its personalization of the past.

In Donna Perry's study of *Annie John*, storytelling is seen as Annie's source of resistance against patriarchal tyranny, after which Helen Tiffin contrasts Kincaid with Erna Brodber, in the way in which each defends the female body's integrity through the art of recitation.

In the book's final essay, Helen Pyne Timothy traces Kincaid's "complex moral cosmology," which she transcends and yet also sustains.

Introduction

Most of the published criticism of Jamaica Kincaid has stressed her political and social concerns, somewhat at the expense of her literary qualities. That is inevitable at this time, but fashions change, and Kincaid will not always be esteemed primarily upon ideological grounds. Her second book, *Annie John* (1985), so far remains her best (in my judgment), but this writer just in her forties is likely to go beyond her earlier work. "Girl" (1984) is one of her briefest stories; I have commented upon it elsewhere and return to it here both because of my affection for its prose and also because it qualifies the critical emphases upon her writing. Ideologues insist that Kincaid has broken with all Western canonical standards, which they associate with such patriarchal malefactors as Shakespeare, Milton, and Dante. Were this true, Kincaid's audience would consist of academic feminists and postcolonial rebels. Since her public is rather larger than that, it is likely that Kincaid's fictions, however original, extend canonical traditions even while attempting to subvert them, which is one of the oldest and most prevalent of literary procedures. Here is my favorite paragraph from "Girl":

> This is how you grow okra—far from the house, because okra tree harbors red ants; when you are growing dasheen, make sure it gets plenty of water or else it makes your throat itch when you are eating it; this is how you sweep a corner; this is how you sweep a whole house; this is how you sweep a yard; this is how you smile to someone you don't like too much; this is how you smile to someone you don't like at all; this is how you smile to someone you like completely; this is how you set a table for tea; this is how you set a table for dinner; this is how you set a table for dinner with an important guest; this is how you set a table for lunch; this is how you set a table for breakfast; this is how you behave in the presence of men who don't know you very well,

1

and this way they won't recognize immediately the slut I have warned you against becoming; be sure to wash every day, even if it is with your own spit; don't down to play marbles—you are not a boy, you know; don't pick people's flowers—you might catch something; don't throw stones at blackbirds, because it might not be a blackbird at all . . .

The fantasy narratives we associate with the literature of childhood frequently have employed a prose poetry akin to Kincaid's highly evocative chant. The girl's voice, speaking to itself, repeats the oppressive mother's litany of admonitions, with the rhythms of repetition shrewdly working to protest the mother's authority. This mode of travesty is fundamental to much of children's literature, whenever the relatively helpless child has to sustain impositions and injunctions. Kincaid's style here is highly individual, but it recalls many narratives in which a young girl at once submits to and yet undermines parental codes of behavior. In some ways, Twain's Huck Finn provides a large analogue, since he adopts the language of the adult world while keeping firmly to a stance all his own. Kincaid's intricate blend of overt submission and implicit defiance repeats (with great skill) immemorial Western modes in which a child's voice wins out over the stale continuities of adult authority.

Kincaid's fierce protest against "touristic" values has its own value and integrity, but would not engage much of her readership if it were not allied to a considerable art of storytelling, and to a prose poetry capable of sustained eloquence. Passionate sincerity, like ideological correctness, is not in itself a *literary* virtue. Fortunately, Kincaid transcends many critical accounts of her achievement to date. She is a stylist and a visionary, and imaginatively is essentially a fantasist. So far, her best work has emerged from recollections of childhood and of her complex relationship to her mother. Her current meditations upon gardening have implicit in them a new development in her work, which her admirers, common readers and critics together, are likely to welcome.

GIOVANNA COVI

Jamaica Kincaid and the Resistance to Canons

Derrida in *Positions* speaks of the necessity of ridding oneself of a metaphysical concept of history, that is linear and systematic. His claim is for a new logic of repetition and *trace*, for a monumental, contradictory, multilevelled history in which the *différance* that produces many differences is not effaced. Jamaica Kincaid's *At the Bottom of the River* and *Annie John* represent examples of writing that break through the objective, metaphysical linearity of the tradition. At the same time, her voice manages to speak up for her specificity without—in so doing—reproducing in the negative the modes of classical white patriarchal tradition. Kincaid's voice is that of a woman and an Afro-Caribbean/American and a post-modern at the same time. This combination is therefore not only disruptive of the institutional order, but also revolutionary in its continuous self-criticism and its rejection of all labels. Perhaps we could say that it is a voice coming *after* the struggles of the women's movement first for recognition and then for separation; the voice of the third "new generation of women" as Kristeva defines it: an effort to keep a polyphonic movement in process in the attempt to be always already questioning and dismantling a fixed metaphysical order, together with a determination to enter history. Her narrative, in fact, is a continuous attempt to turn away from any definitive statement *and* to utter radical statements.

But together with Julia Kristeva in *Unes femmes*, I would ask whose

From *Out of the Kumbla: Caribbean Women and Literature*. © 1990 by Africa World Press.

interest is it to have every woman speak like any other woman; what's the gain? Traditionally our language has been 'silence' because of the yet unshaken authority of the discourse of a sexist order. Under conditions of slavery, black women's creativity was often expressed through the art of quilting: does this history of repression imply that we should necessarily confine our voices within the boundaries traced for us by a patriarchal and racist law? Is the imitation of the language of our oppressor and a total rejection of our historical heritage the only alternative? If the 'universal' of minority literature has been its marginality—as Jan Mohamed maintains—if the Invisible Man had to celebrate his invisibility and define himself through it—now that Black literature is slowly being admitted into the canon, its criticism must resist the hegemonic pressures which seek to neutralize it by repressing its political nature, by levelling its discourse through a rational, apolitical, humanistic criticism. There, where the broken rhythm of jazz is a cry of protest against the symmetry of the racist division of society, or the autobiographical 'intrusions' and 'loss of control' of the narrator in a woman's novel serves as a voice of the private cracking into the authoritative objectivity of the public order, we now risk to find only a conformity to the catechism of one of the many new churches of literature.

The contemporary philosophical debate is increasingly developing around the theme of the crisis of reason. Since Einstein's relativity theory, through Heidegger, Wittgenstein and Nietzsche, and psychoanalysis, but not without the Marxist and Feminist contribution, the metaphysical tradition of the centrality of the Subject is being questioned in stronger and stronger terms. A generic label used to describe this cultural atmosphere is the controversial and too fashionable 'postmodernism.' In literature, it refers to a negative thinking which has resulted in a questioning of the authority of the author (e.g., Barthes, Borges, Eco, Nabokov) and of the fiction/reality relationship (e.g., Pynchon, Coover, Calvino). Despite the disagreement on the denomination (suggested alternatives to 'postmodern literature' range from the apolitical 'metafiction', James Rothner's 'parafiction,' Raymond Federman's 'surfiction,' to the most recent and more politically oriented coinage suggested by Susan Strehle of 'actualism,' among others), in the U.S. critics are defining this avant-garde as almost exclusively white and male. If the postmodern claim to represent an attack against the Western tradition is acceptable as a fact, then how does one account for the absence of the voices of the minorities? Therefore we must question the tendency to take for granted the radicality of the postmodern ideology. Being cognizant that postmodernism itself has already been coopted into a canon that excludes and excommunicates, it wouldn't be surprising to discover that there are in fact postmodern minority writers. I will argue that the connotation of political radicalism associated with postmodernism is acceptable in so far as it opens up to include the specificity of those voices which have been historically discriminated against. I contend that Jamaica Kincaid, a black woman writer, is *radically* postmodern precisely because she is *also* postmodern, but not only so. Her voice, in fact, dismantles the symmetry of the metaphysical tradition in that it escapes all attempts to become domesticated under any label.

The main theme of her writings is the inquiry into the feminine role and racial difference. Kincaid criticizes the very existence of sexual and racial difference, rather than the modes of their existence: there's no place left for reform, the change that is invoked is not one of guards, but of structure.

In *At the Bottom of the River*, at the end of "Girl" we are left with nothing else but a series of imperatives—from "wash the white clothes" to "always eat your food" (*BR*, p. 3)—interrupted by one accusatory question—"is it true that you sing benna in Sunday school?"—, followed by a list of prohibitions—from "don't sing benna" to "don't eat fruits" (*BR*, p. 3)—and by a list of directions—"this is how to sew on a button" to "this is how to behave in the presence of men" (*BR*, p. 4)—,then a few more prohibitions—"don't squat down", "don't throw stones"—and more directions culminating in, "this is how to make ends meet" (*BR*, p. 5). This is a prelude to the final condemnation of the girl as " a slut," not surprising in a story that is almost a 'chronicle of a slut foretold.' The list is spun out at the beat of drums, which provides the only comment to the message that, in a world in which "ends" are means to "meet," girls are "bent on becoming sluts." The practice of making ends meet is the primary target of this ferocious critique which manages to expose the very origin of sexual role division—the rationality of an ideology of symmetry. The 'uncivilized' Lack-of-Reason—the sound of the African drums that beat within the lines—serves as a political commentary, as a cry of protest against the predetermined destiny of the girl.

Particularly fascinating is the story "Blackness" in which the disruption of binary oppositions is devastating: everything is ambiguous, multiple, fragmented. Blackness is the night that "falls in silence" as well as the racial color that "flows through [her] veins" (*BR*, p. 46), but above all it is what cannot be defined—a signifier that escapes its signified by a continuous shifting, "for I see that I cannot see" (*BR*, p. 46). It is identity together with annihilation of the self, "I am swallowed up in the blackness so that I am one with it . . . " (*BR*, p. 47). And the self is "powerful" at the moment when the "I" is "not at one with [it]self," and can say, "I felt myself separate." (*BR*, p. 47). This story ends in a crescendo that is a celebration of the narrative "I," but what kind of "I" is it who ends its song with the words, "I am no longer 'I'" (*BR*, p. 52)? "Blackness" disrupts the concept of identity as One—of phallic identity. Like the ambivalence of the mother's body that is One *and* Other at the same time (herself and the child she bears), this "I" can say: "the blackness cannot be separated from me but often I can stand outside it . . . blackness is visible and yet it is invisible" (*BR*, p. 46). It is neither the silence of the repressed Slave, nor the voice of the Master because, like "the silent voice," "conflict is not part of its nature" (*BR*, p. 52). And her child can stand in front of the mirror looking at her skin without color (*BR*, p. 49), while the "I" is "at last at peace," "at last erased" (*BR*, p. 52), living in the oxymoron of the silent voice.

Open, fragmentary, multiple and paradoxical is also the "frightening" "I" that, "like an ancient piece of history," "will leave room for theories" (*BR*, p. 24) in the story "Wingless." It is at the same time "unaware," "defenseless and pitiful" (*BR*, p. 23), "primitive and wingless," and yet it has the strength to declare:

> I shall grow up to be a tall, graceful, and altogether beautiful woman, and I shall impose on large numbers of people my will and also, for my own amusement, great pain. But now. I shall try to see clearly. I shall try to tell differences. (*BR*, p. 22)

In the future—like the panoptic eye of the omniscient narrator of the logocentric tradition that can see from the God like vantage point of above the world—she will "tell differences" and impose "great pain." The same "I" in the same story is, like her hands, "brown on this side, pink on this side" (*BR*, p. 27).

The questioning of the unity of the self reaches its climax towards the end of the collection:

> I stood as if I were a prism, many-sided and transparent, refracting and reflecting light as it reached me, light that never could be destroyed. And how beautiful I became. (*BR*, p. 80)

This is possible because it is set in the maternal context that blurs—as the lips of the female sex—the distinction between open and closed: "I saw a world in which the sun and the moon shone at the same time" (*BR*, p. 77). The maternal perspective overcomes the nihilism deriving from the dread that faces the contemporary man after—in Lacan's words—"the phallus has been unveiled and exposed to shame":

> For stretching out before him is a silence so dreadful, a vastness, its length and breadth and depth immeasurable. Nothing. (*BR*, p. 68)

The tremendous strength of Kincaid's stories lies in their capacity to resist all canons: They move at the beat of drums and the rhythm of jazz, so that we may be tempted to coopt them under the label of Black Aesthetics as formulated by Amiri Baraka. Yet, sometimes the feeling is more like that of a nursery rhyme—we listen to what Elisabetta Rasy has theorized as 'feminine language': the nurse's language of sounds and silence which stands before and beyond the rational signifying words of the father. The language of the mother and child is expressed by Jamaica Kincaid in the story "My Mother" in these terms:

> My mother and I wordlessly made an arrangement—I sent out my beautiful sighs; she received them. (*BR*, p. 56)

All these stories are structured around the figure of the mother: the writer is constantly connecting artistic creativity to maternity in the effort to create a new representation of the feminine which includes the logic of maternal love. The commitment to this new ethics moves in the direction supported, among others, by Julia Kristeva and Luce Irigaray: bringing the maternal into the discourse of the father represents the new voice outside the dichotomy of sexual difference.

And again there is one more label tempting the critic: under the influence of Gates's formulation of 'signifying' as the main feature of Black Aesthetics, one could conclude that *At the Bottom of the River* is a successful example of this Afro-American rhetorical strategy. Parody, repetition, inversion mark every single movement of Kincaid's narrative.

To add one more and last side to the "prism" of the new self, one could note the insistent refusal to stick to a definitive statement, by going back to the beginning again and again. "What I Have Been Doing Lately" ends where it begins and re-begins in the middle of its non-linear movement (*BR*, p. 43). Like in Coover's *Spanking the Maid* the ultimate order/meaning is never reached:

> On the sides of the deep hole I could see things written, but perhaps it was in a foreign language because I couldn't read them. (*BR*, p. 42)

And so the "I" reverses itself and turns to the maternal horizon: "I said, 'The earth has thin lips,' and I laughed" (*BR*, p. 42).

Kincaid's narrator "doesn't know anymore," she has "no words right now for how [she] feel[s]" (*BR*, p. 30), "no name for the thing [she] had become" (*BR*, p. 80). Yet, she manages to voice her NO in thunder to the existing order of things: "I said, I don't like this. I don't want to do this anymore" (*BR*, p. 45). Yet, she manages to find the strength and take the responsibility to relate to *this* from which she couldn't otherwise escape— she realizes—but through annihilation (*BR*, p. 81). Since nihilism, though cherished, is rejected, a strong and yet unauthoritative voice concludes the whole collection:

> how bound up I know I am to all that is human endeavor, to all that is past and to all that shall be, to all that shall be lost and leave no trace. I claim these things then—mine—and now feel myself grow solid and complete, my name filling up my mouth (*BR*, p. 82)

It doesn't surprise, therefore, that the reviews show a great deal of uneasiness with *At the Bottom of the River*. Edith Milton finds "Miss Kincaid's penchant for apocalyptic imagery disturbing" and believes that "her imagery may be too personal and too peculiar to translate into any sort of sensible communication"; for Anne Tyler the stories are "almost insultingly obscure"; Suzanne Freeman defines the writing as "quirky enough to challenge our very definition of what a short story should be" and notes that the risk is that very few readers may be willing to "decipher the secrets". Unquestionably, the judgement belongs to the audience, but why should we pose this as so dumb? Anne Tyler accuses Kincaid of not "leaning forward and taking our hands and telling us a story"—should critics blame it on the authors if readers need to be taken by their hands? Some readers might prefer to engage in a discourse with the text, rather than joining a "Church-Book" where the "Priest-Author" reveals the Truth.

The reviews of *Annie John* are altogether more positive, but one wonders whether the different evaluation is not simply due to a different reading, rather than to a difference between the two books. While the critics of the first book seemed to be preoccupied with the question of whether the collection worked *as* short stories, the reviewers of *Annie John* entirely over-look the question of the determination of the literary genre to the point that John Bemrose calls it a "collection," Bruce Van Wyngarden takes it for granted that it is a novel, and for Patricia O'Connor it is an autobiographical narrative. All three praise the way it depicts life in Antigua and the coming-of-age of the protagonist.

O'Connor reports the author stating, "the way I became a writer was that my mother wrote my life for me and told it to me." She informs us that Jamaica Kincaid is from Antigua, which she left at seventeen, like Annie John, and her father, too, was a carpenter. In addition, both her mother and her daughter are called Annie. We have no reason to question the definition of Annie John's material es 'autobiographical'—but what kind of 'autobiographical' writing is it? Indeed, it is hard to decide between 'collection' and 'novel', since the book, divided into eight "Chapters," is in fact divided into eight sections each with its own title and internal unity of plot, although their first-person narrative and protagonist is always the same and the setting remains the island of Antigua throughout.

Chapter Three provides us with a clue to interpret what Jamaica Kincaid means by autobiographical writing, an "essay" in this case written for class by the twelve year-old Annie: a metaphor of the entire "novel," it shows how " lies" must enter autobiography when this is meant for a public audience (*AJ*, p. 45). Exactly like *Annie John*, it focuses on Annie and her mother and opens with the description of the paradisiacal Imaginery pre-Oedipal period when the child believes herself to be part of the mother. This union is represented in the image of swimming in the sea: the mother was a "superior" swimmer while Annie "was sure [she] was drowning" when the water reached her knees, but she could swim around with her "arms clasped tightly around her [mother's] neck" (*AJ*, p. 42). The mother would "sing a song in a French patois" that Annie didn't understand or she wouldn't say "anything at all," but the daughter could enjoy "all the sounds" of the world by placing her ear against her mother's neck as if it were a sea shell. The second part of the narrative describes the symbolic separation, with the mother on a rock "tracing patterns" and the water between them. The words of the mother cannot pacify Annie's despair: she has a recurrent dream of the mother on the rock "tracing patterns" with the father. "And it must have been amusing, for they would always make each other laugh" (*AJ*, p. 44). The story is then a metaphor of the Oedipal crisis with the father splitting up the dyadic unity between child and mother and the coming into existence of the speaking subject as a consequence of the desire for the lost mother. It is, in other words, the entrance into the Symbolic which Annie cannot yet accept. Therefore, she imposes a fictional closure to her autobiographical essay: she has her mother shed tears and hold her, rather than simply speak, in order to soothe her anxiety. This "lie" is a return to the repressed union of the "old days," a hiding of the "bad" side of reality. Autobiography, in Jamaica Kincaid's writing, manages to give us a feminist voice that stresses personal experience over the authoritarian universal, without, in so doing, resulting in a demand for realism over modernism, or a poetic discourse, and posing the author as the transcendental signifier of the text, as its meaning and origin.

The pre-Oedipal unity in which the selves of mother and daughter are undifferentiated is the paradise of the first two Chapters of *Annie John*, before the "young-lady business" (*AJ*, p. 26):

> As she told me the stories, I sometimes sat at her side, or I would
> crouch on my knees behind her back and lean over her shoulder.
> As I did this, I would occasionally sniff at her neck or behind her
> ears, or at her hair. She smelled sometimes of lemons, sometimes
> of sage, sometimes of roses, sometimes of bay leaf. At times I
> would no longer hear what it was she was saying; I just liked to
> look at her mouth as it opened and closed over words, or as she
> laughed. (*AJ*, p. 22)

The narrative keeps interrogating the relationship with the mother, also after
"all this was finished" (*AJ*. p. 32) and after the realization that, despite the
same name, the two of them are two separate selves—"She was my mother,
Annie; I was her daughter, Annie" (*AJ*, p. 105), even after the mother has
become "just a dot in the matchbox-size launch swallowed up in the big blue
sea" (*AJ*, p. 148). "It doesn't matter what you do or where you go, I'll always
be your mother and this will always be your home" (*AJ*, p. 47), says the
mother in the end. The caring and nurturing mother is always there when we
need her, even if we can't explain her presence, like the grandmother, Ma
Chess who comes and goes "on a day when the steamer was not due in port"
(*AJ*, p. 127), mysteriously.

    The duality and non-linear temporality of the maternal cannot be
comprehended by the causal discourse of history. Luce Irigaray, in *Ethique de
la différence sexuelle*, notes that sexual difference rests on the interdependence
between space and time: in the beginning was the creation of space, outside
the subject-God who is time itself that materializes in the places of his own
creation. Time is then interior to the subject; space is outside it. The femi-
nine-maternal, being the place of creation, the container for the baby and the
man, becomes deprived of her own place-identity-self. The consequent question is then, "How to figure the place of the place?" Traditionally, the woman
has been *given* a place: the house within whose walls she has been confined.
In *Annie John*, Ma Chess refuses this house of the patriarchal discourse and in
so doing refuses to be placed within the symbolic order of sexual opposition:

> A house? Why live in a house? All you need is a nice hole in the
> ground, so you can come and go as you please. (*AJ*, p. 126)

As Kristeva theorizes in her essay, the time of feminine subjectivity is
either cyclical or monumental—the repetition of biological cycles and the
myth of the archaic Mother—rather than linear—historical. For a redefini-
tion of sexual difference outside the traditional dichotomy, it is necessary to
reconcile these separate conceptions of time and to redefine the time-space

relationship. *Annie John* plays with realistic objective temporality: the adverbial phrase, "On the Sunday before the Monday" (*AJ*, p. 29) is the most visible example of the mocking of spatialized temporality operating within a narrative that never refers to a time outside that of its own story. There are no dates in this autobiographical 'novel', but only the age of the protagonist: rather than a universal interpretation of history, we have "a conversation piece":

> The rain went on in this way for over three months. By the end of it, the sea had risen and what used to be dry land was covered with water and crabs lived there. In spite of what everyone said, the sea never did go back to the way it had been, and what a great conversation piece it made to try and remember what used to be there where the sea now stretched up to. (*AJ*, p. 109)

Also the theme of colonialism is treated by deconstructing the Master-Slave dialectics upon which it rests: After mocking the English who didn't wash often enough—"Have you ever noticed how they smell as if they had been bottled up in a fish?" (*AJ*, p. 36); after having the English girl wear the dunce cap in class; after stressing that "our ancestors"—the "slaves"—"had done nothing wrong except sit somewhere, defenseless," she refuses to appropriate the Western conception of nation in order to express her anti-colonialism and notes:

> Of course, sometimes, what with our teachers and our books, it was hard for us to tell on which side we really now belonged— with the masters or the slaves—for it was all history, it was all in the past, and everybody behaved differently now (*AJ*, p. 76),

not without adding with revolutionary strength that,

> if the tables had been turned we would have acted differently; I was sure that if our ancestors had gone from Africa to Europe and come upon the people living there, they would have taken a proper interest in the Europeans on first seeing them, and said, 'How nice,' and then gone home to tell their friends about it. (*AJ*, p. 76)

This discussion is placed in the context of the wonderful fifth Chapter, where under the picture of "Columbus in Chains" Annie prints in Old English lettering, "The Great Old Man Can No Longer Just Get Up and Go. "She will have to copy Books I and II of *Paradise Lost* for punishment. However, this does not prevent the book from ending with Annie leaving Antigua for England "forever."

Just like the imagery of death which pervades the "paradise" of the first chapters and dissolves as the problems rise in the central part of the book, everything is looked at in its multiple aspects. Grounded on personal experience, Jamaica Kincaid's writing nonetheless defies a realistic interpretation of her voice; it challenges any possibility of deciphering a single meaning by emphasizing multiplicity in what Roland Barthes would call,

> an anti-theological activity, an activity that is truly revolutionary since to refuse to fix meaning is, in the end, to refuse God and his hypostases—reason, science, law.

But for Jamaica Kincaid it certainly does not mean to refuse love as we can know it.

> When I write I don't have any politics. I am political in the sense that I exist. When I write, I am concerned with the human condition as I know it.

LAURA NIESEN DE ABRUNA

Family Connections: Mother and Mother Country in the Fiction of Jean Rhys and Jamaica Kincaid

For the generation of Caribbean women writing in the 1980s and into the 1990s, literary foremothers are such writers as Phyllis Shand Allfrey and Jean Rhys, the latter the better writer of the two. This essay will explore the notion of the 'colonial motherland' in terms of literary inheritance, particularly the influence of one of the pioneer writers, Jean Rhys, on one of the fine contemporary writers, Jamaica Kincaid. Rhys is a foremother in the sense that her presentation of the full range of women's experience is rarely found in the writing of male or female writers, even in the Caribbean, with its predominately matrifocal family. Full female experience, or even the different perspectives provided by women characters, has begun to be presented only in the work of a very few women writers. In the Caribbean, Jean Rhys is one of the first and one of the best of these authors, both in terms of the formal aesthetic merits of the fiction and the exquisiteness of psychological portrayal. Rhys is the literary mother to the next generation of women writers because she was the first Caribbean woman to create texts dealing with the complex mother-daughter matrix. She was also the first writer to employ modernist narrative devices, such as dreams and associative thinking, as the narrator's strategies of resistance to the dominant culture.

The formal qualities of such texts as *Wide Sargasso Sea*, her best work, are poetic compression, orality and metaphor, as well as interior monologues

From *Family Connections: Mother and Mother Country in the Fiction of Jean Rhys and Jamaica Kincaid* by Laura Niesen de Abruna. © 1991 by Laura Niesen de Abruna.

13

and the importance of dreams and association as representational forms. The primacy of the dream vision ending that novel and the continual use of dreams in *Voyage in the Dark* draw attention to Rhys' modernist use of dreams and to the greater acceptance of dreams as a respected type of reality in the work of women writers. In *Voyage in the Dark* dreams and reveries give the novel its structural principle since the narrator uses these means to return to her past whenever something threatening occurs in her present. The blurring of past and present was a deliberate strategy. In a 1934 letter to Evelyn Scott, Rhys pointed out her desire to make *Voyage in the Dark* a conflation of the present and the past. The novel would show, through the use of dream-like narrative, that the past and the present exist side by side: 'I tried to do it by making the past (the West Indies) very vivid—the present dreamlike downward career of a girl'. Rhys' great contribution to full presentation of female life is her exploration of the mother-daughter bond, and specifically the effects of the loss of maternal matrix. The alienation from the mother becomes a metaphor for the white Creole girl's alienation from the mother culture, England.

An emphasis on the personal area of experience is characteristic of women's writing in many cultural contexts. In their recent anthology entitled *Her True-True Name*, Betty Wilson and Pamela Mordecai testify to a flowering in the 1980s of women's writing dealing with such concerns as surviving sexism, negotiating mother-daughter relationships and an interest in relational interaction, or 'bonding'. Most of this literature is concerned, as Evelyn O'Callaghan points out, with bringing the 'personal (private, emotional issues) into the public arena (literature)' (p. 147). In her and Merle Collins' anthology of black women writers, *Watchers & Seekers: Creative Writing by Black Women*, Rhonda Cobham argues for the centrality of either bonding or the absence of bonding in the texts of Caribbean women writers, especially in the literary focus on emotional inter-dependence of mothers and daughters, granddaughters and grandmothers, friends and sisters:

> Their perspectives may be critical, nostalgic or celebratory, sentimental or distanced. But repeatedly there emerges a sense of sisterly solidarity with mother figures, whose strengths and frailties assume new significance for daughters now faced with the challenge of raising children and/or achieving artistic recognition in an environment hostile to the idea of female self-fulfillment. (p. 6)

These are the very issues that Rhys was the first to explore in her fiction, so that every Caribbean writer is in this sense the literary descendant of Rhys.

Suggesting a literary mother-daughter link between Rhys and Kincaid is problematic because there are major differences between the two in terms of race and class interests in their work. Although critics have recognised the aesthetic merits of her fiction, Rhys has not been fully accepted as a West Indian writer because she was a white Creole whose family came from the planter class. Yet a rejection of the formal beauty and the power of the female Creole voice in Rhys' fiction is unwise and untenable. Rhys is a major voice in West Indian writing and has exerted much influence on the younger generation of women writers.

Rhys functions as a literary mother to Kincaid because both authors focus so intensely on the relationship between mothers and daughters and the consequences of the lack of this relationship. In both authors' works, there is a correlation between the political difficulties afflicting the island-'mother' country relationship and the problems affecting the mother-daughter family relationship. In both cases, the characters' separation from the mother or the 'mother' country evokes extreme anxiety that appears as cultural and psychic alienation. In Rhys' writing, especially her novels *Voyage in the Dark* and *Wide Sargasso Sea*, it is the absence of an affirming mother or an affirming 'mother' country that causes dislocation and alien-ation, and ultimately speaks to the importance of such bonds. A later writer like Jamaica Kincaid uses the mother-daughter relationship as her major focus, and also the daughter culture-mother culture bond in a much more direct way (in *Annie John* for example), because Rhys had already prepared the way through her fiction.

To demonstrate this indebtedness of child to mother text, I propose to look at Jean Rhys' first novel, *Voyage in the Dark* (1934), and Jamaica Kincaid's first novel *Annie John* (1983). Both novels concern a young woman's struggle to achieve an identity based on the West Indian cultural experience. Both Anna (*Voyage in the Dark*) and Annie (*Annie John*) experi-ence great tensions in their relationships with their mothers: Annie because of the early intensity of the bond, and Anna because of the complete sever-ance of that bond. In both novels, the importance of female bonding is central and centred in the character's relationship with her mother. In both texts, the character's personal alienation is explored directly and then as a metaphor for the alienation of the daughter-island from the mother-country. The metaphorical exploration offers a criticism of the neo-colonial attitudes that inhibit the lives of both Annie and Anna. Both women are victims of their environments since Anna experiences real or near-death in the abortion scene at the end of the novel, and Annie experiences a long mental break-down just before deciding to leave for England. Both Anna and Annie are forced by family circumstances to leave their islands and attempt to find new lives. At the end of *Annie John*, Annie can find her own identity, signalled through her calling on her own name. She is able to do this through her identification with her mother and her grandmother, Ma Chess, who fills the maternal role when Annie's mother can no longer cope with her illness. In *Voyage in the Dark*, in contrast, Anna's slide towards prostitution and then into a botched abortion and death (at least in the original manuscript) testifies to her inability to find that speaking self, that identified self Annie is able to locate. Anna's complete alienation and destruction may be due to her amorphous status as a white Creole attempting to negotiate an identity in England. Not having been accepted in either the black community in her own island, or the white British community in England, Anna really has no identity except as alien. Annie, on the other hand, will probably survive the trip to England because she is less divided in both her cultural and her personal identity. While it is the literary daughter character Annie who is more successful than the older character Anna, the significance of the first character cannot be underestimated. The story of divisions in self-concept and in cultural identity as experienced by West Indian women was told first by Jean Rhys. In particular, Rhys' first novel *Voyage in the Dark* creates a clear space for the concerns of another specific novel, Jamaica Kincaid's *Annie John*.

Jean Rhys' fiction is often autobiographical in inspiration. While the female narrators of *Voyage in the Dark*, *Anna Morgan*, and *Wide Sargasso Sea*, Antoinette Cosway, are clearly not Rhys herself, the ruptures in mother-daughter bonds suffered by Anna and Antoinette are similar to the personal experiences of Rhys as a young woman. Rhys has provided evidence in both her letters, collected by Francis Wyndam and Diana Melly, and in her unfinished autobiography *Smile Please*, that her link with her mother was strained and eventually severed after Rhys moved to England. Rhys' mother, Minna Lockhart Williams, was apparently a reserved woman who neglected her daughter and completely ignored her after Jean reached puberty. Teresa O'Connor quotes a section of Rhys' unpublished journal, known as the 'Black Exercise Book', that indicates maternal abuse: 'My mother beat me ["whipped me severely" is inserted above the line] I was fond of her but somewhere in my heart I despised her' (f. 12). (Quoted in O'Connor, p. 22.) In fact, O'Connor argues that the unresolved nature of Rhys' relationship with her mother was the force drawing her back to the island of Dominica, or the myth of Dominica, throughout her life and explains why her final and best work takes place in the Caribbean (p. 10).

The facts of Anna Morgan's life parallel those of Jean Rhys' own life. In 1907, at the age of seventeen, Ella Gwendolen Rees, later to be known as

Jean Rhys, left Dominica and emigrated to England. After two years spent in school and on stage she met a considerably older man and stopped working. After the end of the affair, she was left alone to cope with an unwanted pregnancy and a botched abortion. Rhys almost died, but when she recovered she began writing compulsively about the affair in an exercise notebook, later called the 'Black Exercise Book'. The original indicates that the first title of *Voyage in the Dark* was 'Two Tunes', which indicates the shifts of the novel from Anna Morgan's present life in England in 1914 to her past life on an island that is clearly Dominica. As in *Wide Sargasso Sea*, there is in *Voyage in the Dark* a prominent role given to dreams and their ability to carry meaning. For Rhys the dream-like feeling of the novel is a way of conflating the past and the present. Although it was not published until two decades after it was written, Rhys later claimed often that it was her favourite novel (quoted in O'Connor, p. 7), probably because it delved into the same intense layer of autobiography as did *Wide Sargasso Sea* but did so earlier and in a less mediated form.

Deprivation of the mother and emigration to England are also the fate of Anna Morgan, whose life is similar to that of Rhys. Anna leaves Dominica to attend school in England, under the guardianship of her stepmother. After her father's death Anna leaves school and joins a chorus group. She meets Walter Jeffries, a considerably older man, and falls into a sexual liaison that is destructively based on her dependence and his dominance and exploitation.

Critics and readers have been puzzled about the breakdown that Anna experiences after Walter Jeffries leaves her. Even more important is the paralysis that she has suffered because of inadequate strength of ego, which is related to inadequate mothering. When she realises that she has been abandoned she is consumed with a fear that is out of proportion to the event:

> And I saw that all my life I had known that this was going to happen, and that I'd been afraid for a long time, I'd been afraid for a long time. There's fear, of course, with everybody. But now it had grown, it had grown gigantic; it filled me and it filled the whole world.

After their meeting she decides to tell him that she does not want money but simply to see him again: 'You think I want more than I do. I only want to see you sometimes, but if I never see you again I'll die. I'm dying now really, and I'm too young to die' (p. 97). This feeling is linked immediately to the death of her mother, since her subsequent and impulsive reverie is about a funeral in Dominica, with voices murmuring that the deceased was too young to die

(p. 97). When begging Jeffries does no good, Anna imagines herself as being drowned, a figure looking out from underneath the water, her face like a mask.

After Jeffries abandons her, Anna drifts into prostitution and becomes pregnant. She tries to arrange for an abortion, but is caught in a typical 1914 situation—no one but a hack is willing to perform such an operation. The novel's original ending shows Anna dying as a doctor attempts to remedy the botched, illegal abortion she has endured. When Rhys submitted the novel to her publishers, Constable, the editors disapproved of ending the novel with Anna's abortion and death. They insisted that she rewrite it. Under constraint, Rhys complied so that in the published version, the version that is still in print, the doctor and Anna's friend Laurie are laughing as he is attending Anna. Anna's words are:

> When their voices stopped the ray of light came in again under the door like the last thrust of remembering before everything is blotted out. I lay and watched it and thought about starting all over again. And about being new and fresh. And about mornings, and misty days, when anything might happen. And about starting all over again, all over again . . . (pp. 187–88)

The original version of the manuscript indicates that Anna dies during this last scene. The final paragraph of the manuscript reads:

> And the concertina-music stopped and it was so still, so still and lovely like just before you go to sleep and it stopped and there was the ray of light along the floor like the last thrust of remembering before everything is blotted out and blackness comes. (Quoted in O'Connor, p. 129.)

The original ending indicates that Rhys intended that Anna be a young woman without maternal support, exploited by men, who dies in a hostile country. Rhys' own sense of the correctness of her ending is reinforced by the logic of the narrative. The narrative demands Anna's death since only this logically follows Rhys' attempt to make the maternal and colonial deprivations parallel. Anna is killed by the absence of a nurturing mother and of nurturing 'mother' country. Anna drifts into death when her consciousness is 'blotted out', and her voyage from Dominica to England is a voyage into the darkness of death. This voyage into the dark, and out of the light, suggests the way the colonial is treated in the mother country—a coercive and oppressive relationship that is followed by an attempt to control the minds and bodies of those colonised.

This coercion of the colonised, a colonisation of their bodies, is clear during Anna's pregnancy when she compares her situation to being on a ship and then being thrown overboard. When Anna becomes pregnant it appears to be accidental. Almost immediately, she thinks of having an abortion as a way of controlling her situation. Her reveries of what she should do are punctuated with memories of being forced away from her island. She dreams that she is on a ship and:

> From the deck you could see small island—dolls of islands—and the ship was sailing in a dolls' sea, transparent as glass.
>
> Somebody said in my ear, 'That's your island that you talk such a lot about.'
>
> And the ship was sailing very close to an island, which was home except that the trees were all wrong. These were English trees, their leaves trailing in the water. I tried to catch hold of a branch and step ashore, but the deck of the ship expanded. Somebody had fallen overboard. (p. 165)

The heaving of the boat wakes her up and becomes the heaving of her stomach as she suffers nausea. She is the person who has fallen overboard in an alien ocean. The ship has taken her from Dominica to England, the place where the trees are all different. Having been forced away from her island, it has assumed an air of unreality and triviality, like a doll island rather than a human homeland. The social and economic powerlessness she feels in England, the desperate feeling of being trapped by changes in her body, and the deprivation of the maternal matrix represented by the island, are all embodied in this dream.

In *Voyage in the Dark*, as in Rhys' later novels, there is a woman narrator who is deprived of parental nurturing and suffers from this lack of support. Anna's mother has died before the opening of the novel, and her father dies soon after her arrival in England. Her situation is exacerbated because of her political status as a white Creole and her subsequent alienation as a colonial in England. There she becomes a marginal woman living on the money received in exchange for sex. This is a pattern not only in *Voyage in the Dark* but also in all of her novels, in each of which the female character is rejected first by their mothers and then by a male lover, or series of lovers. It appears in all of these novels that the men in positions of power and wealth are the enemy, but the problems of identity and self-esteem for the women characters stem from their inadequate bonding with their mothers. Unable to form a positive self-identity, they are vulnerable to exploitation by men and other women.

The narrative pattern in *Voyage in the Dark* is therefore one of maternal loss and attempted compensation through memory. In these memories, Anna attempts to recapture the island itself, symbol of the mother. Although the memories seem to be reveries out of Anna's control, they form a pattern. Each time Anna suffers loss or humiliation, she returns to thoughts of the island as an unconscious way of deflecting despair through imaginative attachment to the mother. While the projection of such comfort is an admirable strategy against complete dominance by the colonial power, it is inadequate to save Anna, and we must wait for Antoinette Cosway to find a character capable of turning dream compensation into adequate resistance.

Anna's emigration to England was a watershed for her, the breaking off of all possibility of finding connection with the maternal or the maternal island. To indicate this frequent break of past from present, Rhys uses the image of a curtain falling. The novel's first words concern the alienation Anna felt upon arriving in England: 'It was as if a curtain had fallen, hiding everything I had ever known. It was almost like being born again' (p. 7). Here England acts as a negative substitute for the parents, and especially the mother, that Anna has lost in coming to the 'mother' country. In being born again she has lost connection with her biological mother and has re-emerged as a child without parents, as an orphaned consciousness unable to ground itself.

Anna searches for mother substitutes throughout the novel, and her search is represented in terms of images of the island. In the first chapter Anna thinks to herself that an older woman in the chorus, Laurie Gaynor, is the only woman on stage who shows her affection. (And it is Laurie who takes Anna into her home when she needs an abortion.) This act of mother substitution is followed immediately by a memory about Dominica:

> Lying between 15° 10' and 15° 40' N. and 61° 14' and 61° 30' W. 'A goodly island and something highland, but all overgrown with woods,' that book said. And all crumpled into hills and mountains as you would crumple a piece of paper in your hand—rounded green hills and sharply-cut mountains.
> A curtain fell and then I was here. (p. 17)

Anna never adjusts to life in a different country because her problems with her mother are unresolved. She longs for the 'rounded green hills' of the goodly island, a maternal image that reinforces the traditional association of the land and of nature with the female. A falling curtain points to the impossibility of the desired pre-oedipal merging with the mother. A falling curtain also indicates the end of a theatrical presentation, like the one in which Anna is currently engaged, and marks an end rather than a beginning. Coming to England does not indicate the opening of the curtains but their closing, the end of something. The novel does not move forward in time, just as Anna's life does not progress but stagnates in its own despair. Her sexual liaison with Walter Jeffries is not romance but a symptom of stagnation, an attempt to destroy reality: 'You shut the door and you pull the curtain over the windows and then it's as long as a thousand years and yet so soon ended' (p. 79). And, when she closets herself in a new room after the affair and writes about it, she remarks 'I kept the curtains drawn all the time' (p. 104).

A further image associated with the falling curtain is impending blindness, the falling curtain being the image suffered by someone whose retina has become detached by a hard blow to the head. The image is repeated later in the novel to describe the condition of people in marginal positions. The preacher at Marble Arch, dismissed by Maudie as insane, attracts Anna because she respects his understanding, 'because his eyes had a blind look, like a dog when it sniffs something' (p. 48). The image of blindness is also linked with darkness, and darkness with death, leading to the true ending of the novel. In formal terms, the narrative is aborted by the closing of a curtain on the future.

Because there is no future to anticipate, Anna is tempted to compress the past and the present into a dreamlike state that adumbrates the death scene at the end of the novel: 'Sometimes it was as if I were back there and as if England were a dream. At other times England was the real thing and out there was the dream, but I could never fit them together' (p. 8). This confusion of dream and reality is also one of the formal experiments of the novel. Anna is suspended in a static, dreamlike state because she cannot fit past and present together. As she remarks about her experience with Jeffries: 'I got that feeling of a dream, of two things that I couldn't fit together' (pp. 77–78). Because she cannot fit past and present together, there is no possible future for her. Rhys shifts the narrative from straightforward progression to dreamlike sequences throughout the novel to reinforce the idea that Anna is caught in a nightmare state of unreality imposed by her psychological stress.

Throughout the novel Anna meets a series of unforgiving, negative mother figures. Many of them are landlandies, whom Anna regards as surrogate mothers. The first in this series is the landlady who reproves Anna and Maudie for coming downstairs in their nightgowns and robes. Maudie acknowledges the link between reproving landlady and mother directly: '"It's all right, ma," Maudie said. "I'm going up to get dressed in a minute"' (p. 9). Later, when Maudie and Anna bring home Walter Jeffries and his companion, she 'glares' at them, speechless in her disapproval. At her flat in London, Anna's landlady dislikes her receiving flowers and money from a man and tells her to leave: "'I don't want no tarts in my house, so now you know'" (p. 30). Anna describes all of her landladies in detail, but focuses on their reactions to her, thereby giving them judgmental power. After her affair with Jeffries has ended, Anna's new landlady is monstrous: 'This one had bulging eyes, dark blobs in a long, pink face, like a prawn' (p. 103).

Images of the critical mother-landlady are juxtaposed with compensatory dreams of the island. The image of Anna's second landlady is followed by reminiscences of the good mother substitute, Francine, her black nurse in Dominica, who once saved her from a great fear of cockroaches: 'I was happy because Francine was there, and I watched her hand waving the fan backwards and forwards and the beads of sweat that rolled from underneath her handkerchief' (p. 31). In *Smile Please* Rhys speaks of a black woman, Francine, whom she admired and who told stories beginning with a ritual invocation to the obeah god Boisséche. Francine's positive role is carried through into that of Anna's nurse Francine in *Voyage*. Interestingly, Rhys identified her own nurse as a woman named Meta, whom she disliked and feared. According to the account in *Smile Please*, Meta told Rhys enough stories about zombies, soucriants and loup-garous (werewolves) that she claims to have remained marked by fear throughout her life: 'Meta had shown me a world of fear and distrust, and I am still in that world' (p. 24).

Through her identification with Francine, Anna fantasises that she herself is mulatta and attempts to link herself imaginatively with others who have been cast out by the British. She identifies with one of the slaves on her family's old estate, a house servant named Maillotte Boyd, listed in the records as 18 years old, Anna's present age. Anna returns to this identification when she realises that Jeffries considers her a disposable purchase. Then she remembers Maillotte again: '*Maillotte Boyd, aged 18. Maillotte Boyd, aged 18 . . . But I like it like this. I don't want it any other way but this*' (p. 56). She recognises the link between Maillotte and herself since both are women whose bodies are owned by men who can sell them, or buy them off in Anna's case, when they grow tired of them. Anna cannot find any comfort through identification with Francine because the racial barrier prevented a bond that would have been continually nurturing. Despite their good communication, Francine, here more like Rhys' Meta, is ultimately suspicious of Anna because she is white: 'But I knew that of course she disliked me too because I was white; and that I would never be able to explain to her that I hated being white' (p. 72). For the same reason, Maillotte cannot really be a sister substitute.

Despite these problems of identification with oppressed peoples, Anna has some strategies for resistance. Among them is that of aligning poor white women with the black women whose bodies were bartered for money.

Writing, too, is a strategy of resistance, as she re-creates her experience of emotional and financial bondage in her room, in her words, and from her perspective rather than from the male power base represented by Walter Jeffries. Writing allows her to find a connection between herself and the Carib Indians who were never conquered by the Europeans who sought to subdue Dominica: "'The Caribs indigenous to this island were a warlike tribe, and their resistance to white domination, though spasmodic, was fierce . . .." They are now practically exterminated' (p. 105).

Anna's stepmother Hester is the worst of the rejecting mothers, a woman who represents all the pettiness and hostility of all of the landladies and shopkeepers. Without consulting Anna, she had written to Anna's Uncle Ramsay telling him that she should really go back home. Hester has suspected how Anna lives without any visible source of income and eschews responsibility for her behaviour. She writes to her uncle insisting that he pay for half Anna's fare back to Dominica. Ramsay states that Hester has cheated Anna out of the inheritance of the estate since Hester sold it and moved to England without giving Anna any money from the sale. Hester's response to this letter evidences a resentment of the island, her husband, the isolation, weather and the people, about whom she shows a real racism. She turns around the conversation by accusing Anna of whoring: 'Because don't imagine that I don't guess how you're going on. Only some things must be ignored some things I refuse to be mixed up with I refuse to think about even' (p. 63). Hester clearly regards everyone who grew up in Dominica mulatto or black and feels free to reject Anna on that basis alone. She never writes again to Anna, and that is her last communication with the woman who is supposed to be her stepmother. Instead of fighting with her, Anna concedes defeat and hopes that she can live on Jeffries' money.

Ethel Matthews is the final negative mother image in the novel. A victim of British respectability yet unable to support herself, Ethel walks the line between masseuse and madame. She expects Anna to behave in the same way, but Anna does not know British hypocrisy games, nor does she really care enough about her reputation to indulge in duplicity. As if in a strangled mother-daughter dyed, Ethel feels that she both hates Anna, asking her to leave at one time, and also needs her desperately because she is getting old and wants company. At one point she reveals some of her genuine feelings: 'Look here, I'll tell you something. You can clear out. You're no good; I don't want you here' (p. 144). Yet she also begs Anna's forgiveness because she needs her company. When Anna becomes pregnant, Ethel turns sour and writes to Laurie trying to get money, saying that Anna owes two weeks' rent. Ethel had thrown Anna out when she discovered the pregnancy and leaves her to find lodgings with Laurie. Ethel believes that Anna has crossed the line from respectability to tramping:

> It is one thing for a girl to have a friend or two but it is quite another for it to be anybody who she picks up in the street and without with your leave or by your leave and never a word to me. (p. 166)

She ends the complaint by saying that Anna is not someone who will do anything for herself. The unwillingness to privilege self-interest is for Ethel the ultimate obscenity to commit in British culture.

The end of the novel represents Anna's farewell to the mother, the flesh and the island as she prepares to die while dreaming of Carnival. The word 'carnival' derives, of course, from the Latin *carne vale*, meaning farewell to the flesh. Throughout the novel Anna has associated the behaviour of the English with that of the masked carnival players who became inhuman ants or animals in Dominica, where masks were worn by the blacks in order to satirise their white masters. Anna feels that she is the victim of both black and white hatred that is signalled by the mask. The British wear masks without effort or irony; they know how to mask their feelings, how to use one another to 'get on', as Vincent and Walter Jeffries say. The blacks in Dominica use masks once a year to poke fun at the whites, just as Meta did to Anna:

> But most of all I was afraid of the people passing because I was dying; and, just because I was dying, any one of them, any minute, might stop and approach me and knock me down, or put their tongues out as far as they would go. Like that time at home with Meta, when it was Masquerade and she came to see me and put out her tongue at me through the slit in the mask. (p. 178)

At the end of the novel, Rhys introduces a new character, Meta, whom Anna says came specifically to her house, masked, to tease her. It is surprising to see Meta's name where one would have expected Francine's without explanation of this new character who shares a name with Rhys' nurse. Interestingly, Anna mentions Meta here for the first and only time. (In *Smile Please* Meta is, of course, the name of Rhys' nurse, who seems to have been transformed in *Voyage in the Dark* into Francine.) As the emotions intensify for Anna, Rhys seems to revert back to the prototype of the nurse and abandons the name Francine for Meta. Although this may have been an authorial slip, Meta still acts as the final negative mother figure who literally sticks her tongue out at Anna as she is dying.

Meta acts for all Dominican blacks in resenting and then mocking the more powerful whites. The laughing masks and the concertina music are brought together, in synchrony, as Anna is dying. This image leads to the scene in which Anna haemorrhages while the doctor's laughter at her, the scornful mask of the British and the concertina music, played by a black man, announce her death. The death scene also gives the image of a final ray of light that comes into Anna's consciousness, linking this to the idea of blindness and of the curtain falling. In the final scene, Anna is the victim of two things that she cannot put together—her emotional vulnerability caused by a lack of adequate mothering and her victimisation by the 'mother' country.

The mask is a symbol for the text's strategies of resistance. Anna does fight back through telling people what she thinks, through running away from the insensitive Walter Jeffries and, most of all, through her refusal to evaluate all human relationships, especially sexual relationships, in terms of money. Echoing the masked Meta, she even sticks out her tongue at Jeffries when she jams a cigarette on his hand. The text represents her other strategies of resistance through her continual use of dreams to subvert the economic and sexual relationships she is forced into in England. Anna can defy her family and the British, although she is surely also the victim of maternal abuse and the abuse of the 'mother' country. Yet, as the text passes into the hand of the readers, it assumes another mother role. In aligning the reader's sympathies with Anna the text sticks its tongue out at the 'mother' country and unmasks its hostility and anger at the lost maternal matrix and the irresponsible and bigoted behaviour of the imperialistic power. This juxtaposition of the unmasking and taunting of mother and 'mother' country is the centre of the daughter text of *Voyage in the Dark*, Jamaica Kincaid's *Annie John*.

We have known for some time that Jamaica Kincaid writes with a double vision. From one point of view, her early fiction and sketches in *The New Yorker*, her collection of dream visions, *At the Bottom of the River* (1978), and her novel *Annie John* (1983) all concern the coming-of-age narrative of a young woman in Antigua. Much of Kincaid's fiction, especially the intensely lyrical prose poetry of *At the Bottom of the River* and the autobiographical novel *Annie John*, focuses on the relationship between mother and daughter and the painful separation that occurs between them. Careful examination of the psychoanalytical implications of these relationships will surely open up the meanings of these texts. A psychoanalytic analysis from a feminist perspective, one examining mother-daughter bonding, would point out that the narrators in Kincaid's fiction resist separation from the mother as a way of denying their intense fear of death. The fear of separation is further complicated in *Annie John*, because the narrator leaves the island for Britain with the clear intention of making a break with her environment.

Both she and her mother, who is also named Annie, have left their respective mothers and their own homes to seek a more comfortable life elsewhere. The process of Annie's leaving her mother is mirrored in the process of leaving the island. Displacement from an initial intimacy with her mother's realm is reflected in a growing away from the environment until, at the end of the novel, Annie can only dream of leaving her own home for England.

Along with a psychoanalytic-feminist perspective, however, other views must be taken of Kincaid's fiction. *Annie John*, for example, is not just the story about a young woman's involvement with her mother and her home. There is a story behind this story of how and why these conflicts are situated in a West Indian island recently liberated from British rule. The novel is not the story of a white, bourgeois mother and daughter but of an African-Caribbean mother from Dominica and her daughter living in a nine-by-twelve mile island that is drought- and poverty-stricken and far removed from the privileges of middle-class life in Europe or the United States.

That Kincaid thought about these differences when writing her fiction is clear from a 'Talk of the Town' article for *The New Yorker* which appeared in 1977. Kincaid, who rejected her British name Richardson, recalled that most of the African-Caribbean people of Antigua worked as carpenters, masons, servants in private homes, seamstresses, fishermen or dockworkers. She added that, 'A few grew crops and a very small number worked in offices and banks.' When Kincaid was seven she was herself apprenticed to a seamstress for two afternoons a week. People who worked in offices and banks were white, and the most wealthy ran a country club called the Mill Reef Club. The whites owned the banks and the offices and reserved most of the island's pleasant beaches for themselves. This historical and political context is central to Kincaid's fiction.

Much of Kincaid's distrust of the post-colonial environment went unnoticed by the reviewers of *Annie John*. The novel was received as simply a book about mothers and daughters, a popular topic in feminist literary criticism, especially during the late 1970s when Nancy Chodorow and Carole Gilligan each published influential studies. Female bonding is the novel's subject and receives the most narrative attention, whereas within the novel there are only two explicit statements of resentment made about the political or social situations. One is a comment the narrator makes while observing a classmate, Ruth, who is the child of British missionaries:

> Perhaps she wanted to be in England, where no one would remind her constantly of the terrible things her ancestors had done; perhaps she had felt even worse when her father was a missionary in Africa. I could see how Ruth felt from looking at

her face. Her ancestors had been the masters, while ours had been the slaves. She had a lot to be ashamed of . . . I am quite sure that if the tables had been turned we would have acted differently.

Earlier in the novel, while Annie and her friend the Red Girl watch a cruise ship with wealthy passengers go by, she fantasises that they throw them confusing signals and crash the ship: 'How we laughed as their cries of joy turned to cries of sorrow' (p. 71).

Any doubts that there is implicit criticism of the post-colonial Antigua in *Annie John* were erased by the publication of *A Small Place* in 1988. This series of essays externalises Kincaid's resentment of the British upper class and forces us to look at *Annie John* from a different angle. Emphasis shifts to the way Annie constantly rebels against the cultural norms imposed by the British slave owners and the wealthy, like the members of the Mill Reef Country Club. Viewed from the perspective of *A Small Place*, the fantasy of Annie and the Red Girl becomes not a minor incident but the tip of a mass of repressed feelings. The Red Girl allows Annie to explore her true feelings precisely because the Red Girl—and this is her major attraction for Annie— does not participate in any of the 'young lady' or 'proper person' rituals that are imposed on Annie by her school and her mother. The Red Girl refuses to behave in stereotyped roles, especially gender roles, and avoids all the rules and rituals associated with being a 'young lady'.

Resentment of British influence is even clearer in *A Small Place*. There she recites an elegy for an Antigua that no longer exists. The British have ruined much of the island:

> And so everywhere they went they turned it into England; and everybody they met they turned English. But no place could ever really be England, and nobody who did not look exactly like them would ever be English, so you can imagine the destruction of people and land that came from that. The English hate each other and they hate England, and the reason is they have no place else to go and nobody else to feel better than.

At the age of seven Kincaid remembers waiting for hours in the hot sun to see a 'putty-faced princess' from England disappear behind the walls of the governor's house. Later she found out that the princess was sent to Antigua to recover from an affair with a married man. In both the schools and libraries, the British found opportunities to distort and erase Antiguan history and to glorify British history in its place. One of the crimes of the colonial era was the violation of the colonised peoples' languages: 'For isn't it odd that the only language I have in which to speak of this crime is the language of the criminal who committed the crime?' (*A Small Place*, p. 31).

The thematic connection between *Annie John* and *A Small Place* became clearer in an interview with Selwyn Cudjoe appearing in *Callaloo*. Kincaid discussed her ideas in *A Small Place*, particularly her dislike of colonialism which she developed by the age of nine:

> When I was nine, I refused to stand up at the refrain of 'God Save Our King'. I hated 'Rule Britannia'; and I used to say that we weren't Britons, we were slaves. I never had any idea why. I just thought that there was no sense to it—'Rule Britannia, Britannia rules the waves, Britons never shall be slaves.' I thought that we weren't Britons and that we were slaves. (p. 397)

Elsewhere in the interview Kincaid indicates an instinctive rebellion she felt concerning England, despite the validation of British culture: ' . . . for us England (and I think this was true for VS Naipaul, too) and its glory was at its most theatrical, its most oppressive. Everything seemed divine and good only if it was English' (p. 398). Although Kincaid eschews an overtly political allegiance, there is a close connection between Kincaid's anti-colonialist essays in *A Small Place* and the feeling ascribed to the young narrator of *Annie John*. The attitudes expressed explicitly in *A Small Place* are implicit in *Annie John*.

Thus, when we talk about the women characters in Kincaid's fiction, especially *Annie John*, we must talk not only about the autobiographical experiences, but also about the life of a young and brilliant African-Caribbean woman from an impoverished neighbourhood on an island that won independence from the 'mother' country. A feminist perspective will remind us that it is absurd to pretend that a novel written by a woman about women will not differ from a novel written by a man about men. However, one must be careful to examine the appropriateness of white, middle-class feminist theory to the texts produced by Caribbean women. Ketu Katrak, among others, has criticised famous literary theorists like Fredric Jameson for their appropriation of post-colonial texts as 'raw material' for the production of literary theories consumed in western academies. Also, as Evelyn O'Callaghan states in an article on the application of feminist theory to Caribbean literature, 'Cross-cultural self-conceptions of men and women appear to be more dramatic than contrasts between those who share the same socio-cultural system' (p. 148). In other words, cultural differences might be as salient as gender difference in interpretation of literary texts. Particularly important is O'Callaghan's suggestion that there are problems for Caribbean women's writing when an over-rigid concept of feminist theory is applied. However, she is in favour of a 'crossroads' model which situates each work at a point of intersection of other concerns with race, class, or Creole cultural forms unique to the region (p. 160). Women's stories will relate the female perspective on these experiences and reflect on any sexist strategies that persist in post-colonial societies.

The critic must take issues of race, post-colonial history, class and gender into consideration as they come up in the literary work. The feminist critic should be careful not to use prescriptive models in interpreting West Indian women's texts. This being the case, we must conclude that Kincaid is writing not with a double vision but a vision that has four perspectives. To look at all of them is beyond the scope of this essay, so I propose to offer a new reading of the ways in which *Annie John* combines the narrator's dissatisfaction with her personal relationships with a dissatisfaction with her post-colonial environment.

In particular, it should be pointed out that in Antigua, and elsewhere, there was much cultural violence directed toward women based on popular attitudes toward their sexuality and their bodies. These attitudes were a combination of Victorian ideology and regressive religious views. Such attitudes spread through the educational system and were widely adopted, sometimes even by the women who were denigrated by these ideologies (Katrak, p. 171). The same system of British education that erased and colonised indigenous history also attempted to erase female sexuality and to control the female body. Attempted colonisation of the female body is one of the points of contention between Annie and her mother because Annie constantly rebels against those aspects of her society that have been imposed by the British. Some of these norms have been absorbed by Annie's neighbours, her school and, especially and unfortunately, by her beautiful, loving and well-intentioned mother. She is not presented negatively but sympathetically as a victim of post-colonial strategies to erase her identity and to substitute European ideology in its place. In *A Small Place* Kincaid calls her mother someone who is suffering from her 'innocence' of white racism (p. 29). There is not a conscious understanding of this on the character Annie's part but simply an uneasy feeling about authority figures.

In *Annie John* the narrator's personal displacement is reflected in a growing away from the environment. The first chapter, in a novel ostensibly about coming of age, ironically concerns death. This is Kincaid's deliberate strategy since the novel is not about a beginning but about the end of the narrator's intimacy with her mother and her island. During a period when she was ten years old, the narrator becomes obsessed with attending funerals.

The displacement and boredom she experienced—she had nothing to do and spoke only to her parents—led her to focus on the only source of activity in the neighbourhood, the cemetery where she would see 'stick-like', three-dimensional figures. After Annie's mother says that these people were attending a funeral, and that children died, Annie became afraid of death. For the first time, the separation of death is connected with her mother: 'My mother knew of many people who had died in such a way. My mother knew of many people who had died, including her own brother' (p. 4). Later, when a neighbour girl dies in her mother's arms, Annie begins to connect her mother's circling arm with death, as if the mother were both the place of protection and the instrument of destruction.

To reinforce this sense of separation, there is a series of lost parental figures. Annie's father was left in Antigua by parents who went to Latin America, leaving him with a grandmother who died when he was 18. When Annie cries at this story, her mother comforts her: 'She said that I needn't worry about such a thing as her sailing off or dying and leaving me all alone in the world' (p. 24). Yet, Annie's mother had also lost her father when she was quite young and was constrained to set out on her own. She was an inde-pendent woman who, at 16, after quarrelling with her father, packed a trunk and left home. When Annie was young the trunk contained things that had belonged to her, starting from just before she was born. Her mother would lift up each object and tell her the story connected with it—a tremendous pleasure for Annie: 'No small part of my life was so unimportant that she hadn't made a note of it, and now she would tell it to me over and over again' (p. 22). Despite the closeness that Annie experiences with both her father and her mother, they consider her old enough to leave the house at 17 or even 16—the age they were when they set out on their own. After this age Annie is not completely welcome in the house.

The most dramatic changes occur for Annie when she turns 12, the summer she reaches puberty and a watershed in her relationship with her mother. She refuses to cut a dress for herself and for Annie from the same material: 'You cannot go around the rest of your life looking like a little me' (p. 26). Annie is devastated: 'It wasn't just what she said, it was the way she said it' (p. 24). Annie feels bitterness and hatred, not for her mother, but for 'life in general' (p. 26), as if realising that her mother could not be blamed for the process of growing into an adult.

Complying with expectations for a proper British lady, Annie's mother abandons the values represented by the trunk and appropriates those of the culture she sees around her. There are many lessons to teach Annie how to behave as a 'young lady'. Annie takes lessons in manners but is sent home because she cannot resist making farting noises when practicing her curtsy.

Likewise, the piano teacher dismisses her because Annie cannot resist eating from a bowl of plums that is on the table. To Annie, the teacher is 'a shriveled-up old spinster from Lancashire, England' (p. 28). Although Annie may be thwarting the lessons because her mother is planning their separation, she is also responding to the tyranny of the lessons themselves and to the cultural values implicit in them.

The problem that definitively sours their intimacy is the older woman's attitudes toward sexuality and the body. Rushing home from Sunday school, Annie returns to the house to hear sounds coming from the bedroom. She focuses on her mother's hand that she sees circling her father's back: 'It was white and bony, as if it had long been dead and had been left out in the elements' (p. 30). The hand signals death to Annie, and here it is the death of her love for her mother. There is also something new in her mother's tone toward her: 'She said in a voice that was sort of cross and sort of something else, "Are you going to just stand there doing nothing all day?"' (p. 31) A few days after this Annie meets a young girl, Gwen, and 'falls in love' with her as a way of compensating for the love she felt had been withdrawn.

Her mother believes that a woman's body is the property of the respectable male who will marry her. Until that time, strict vigilance must be practiced so that one does not appear loose or vulgar. Annie's mother is extremely regressive on this issue, accepting a Victorian ideology that includes the colonisation of the female body. In the story 'Girl' from *At the Bottom of the River* the mother recites a litany of sexual warnings at her daughter:

> On Sundays try to walk like a lady and not like the slut you are
> so bent on becoming . . . this is how to hem a dress when you see
> the hem coming down and so to prevent youself from looking
> like the slut I know you are so bent on becoming . . . this is how
> to behave in the presence of men who don't know you very well,
> and this way they won't recognise immediately the slut I have
> warned you against becoming. (p. 4)

The mother's obsessive refrain of hostility indicates her belief in the necessity of guarding one's sexual virtue if one is to be an unspoiled commodity on the marriage market. In *Annie John* the major explosion between the two women comes from the daughter's sexual coming of age. When she is 15 Annie is looking in the shop windows on Market Street, alone, when she becomes aware of a group of boys laughing at her: 'I knew instantly that it was malicious and that I had done nothing to deserve it other than standing here all alone' (p. 95). She recognises one of the young men and attempts to speak to him, but he and his friends laugh slyly and refuse to treat her as someone worthy of conversation. She remembers playing with this boy when they were younger. Feeling his cruelty on this occasion brings a sharp memory of another incident, the day he persuaded her to take off her clothes and sit beneath a tree where there were many red ants.

Annie's mother sees the conversation with the young men and instantly accuses her daughter of behaving as a 'slut':

> The word 'slut' (in patois) was repeated over and over, until suddenly I felt as if I were drowning in a well but instead of the well being filled with water it was filled with the word 'slut', and it was pouring in through my eyes, my ears, my nostrils, my mouth. (p. 102)

To save herself, Annie is rude to her mother, who replies 'Until this moment, in my whole life I knew without a doubt that, without any exception, I loved you best' (p. 103). There is no going back because this incident strips Annie of her belief in herself and initiates a long mental breakdown. To the extent that Annie's mother accepts bourgeois attitudes toward women's bodies, she will never appreciate her daughter in an uncorrupted way. Like the young boys, she treats Annie as if she were merely a body to be controlled or possessed.

In other parts of the novel Annie's comments and dissatisfactions are responses to the British education that was forced on her, with her mother's approval. In Annie's new classroom, for instance, while the students write autobiographical essays, Miss Nelson reads from an 'elaborately illustrated edition of *The Tempest*' (p. 39), Kincaid's signal that the classroom is another occasion for the imperialist, prosperous Prosperos to force their language and traditions on the indigenous Calibans of the island. During the history lesson recounted in the chapter 'Columbus in Chains', the class reads *The History of the West Indies*, an account written only from the British point of view. A picture of the dejected and miserable Columbus, who was brought back to Spain after his third voyage fettered in chains, sparks Annie's interest: 'What just deserts, I thought, for I did not like Columbus' (p. 77). She is reminded of her own grandfather. He had forced her mother from their home and from Dominica because she wanted to live alone, and he insisted that unmarried women should live with their fathers. On hearing that the old man needed a cane to walk, her mother had exclaimed: 'So the great man can no longer just get up and go' (p. 78), a phrase that Annie musingly associates not only with the patriarchal figure in her family but also with the patriarchal figure in her schoolbook. She writes the phrase under the picture of Columbus.

The grandfather's attempt to control the body of his daughter is similar to the colonials' attempts to own women's bodies. In fact, her grandfather's assumption of control outlasted the coloniser's control of the island as well as any strategies of decolonisation. Annie is punished for her impertinence and disrespect: 'I had gone too far this time, defaming one of the great men in history, Christopher Columbus, discoverer of the island that was my home' (p. 82). As a discipline, she must copy books I and II of *Paradise Lost*, a work that evokes the biblical imagery of a lost Eden in the novel and is suggestive of the snake as coloniser whose poison is circulating through the system.

During one of Miss Nelson's classes the students are asked to write an autobiographical essay. One student discusses an aunt living in England, and her dream of one day moving in with her; another girl told of a brother studying medicine in Canada; someone else had taken tea with Lady Baden-Powell. Annie's composition, the prototype of the novel itself, dealt with her mother: 'What I had written was heartfelt, and, except for the very end, it was all too true' (p. 41). In the essay she tells of the swimming lessons during which she was afraid of the water and would only go into the sea on her mother's back. When she cannot find her mother one day, 'A huge black space then opened up in front of me and I fell inside it' (p. 43). Her mother finds her and tells her that she will never leave her: 'And though she said it over and over again, and though I felt better, I could not wipe out of my mind the feeling I had had when I couldn't find her' (p. 44). The other girls concoct stories that reflect the corruption of their desires and dreams. They want to go to England, Canada or, at least, have tea with a noblewoman from Britain. Annie, on the other hand, feels the gulf that separates her from the others, specifically her mother, and tells of falling into a black depression.

Her final fantasy, her mother telling her that no separation will occur, is incorrect in two ways. Annie's mother is assiduously preparing her daughter for the separation that will assuredly occur since her parents want the grown Annie to create her own household. In addition, Annie will always feel a gulf separating her from her own island. The classroom scenes suggest that the island's inappropriate education provides one of the worst forms of alienation. Yet, her mother completely approves of this British cultural imperialism. Annie's mother is well intentioned and watches out for her child, hoping to give her opportunities she did not have. But she is also carrying within her a type of poison that distracts and threatens Annie.

This tension is conveyed through several images. The mother used to accompany her father into the mountains to gather food. Once, walking down the mountain with a bunch of green figs on her head, she was startled by a huge snake that had hidden itself in the fruit. The snake is the obvious symbol of evil carried in or on the head of the mother. One also thinks of Medusa whose head of snakes turned people to stone, but the connection in Kincaid's mind was more likely through *Paradise Lost*. The poison that

Milton presents is conformity of Creole life to British expectations.

The gap separating Annie from her mother and home becomes an ugly depression when she is 15: 'My unhappiness was something deep inside me, and when I closed my eyes I could even see it . . . it took the shape of a small black ball all wrapped in cobwebs' (p. 84). This depression is completely defined in Annie's mind by her relationship with her mother: 'Something I could not name just came over us, and suddenly I had never loved anyone or hated anyone so' (p. 80). For three months the rains pelted Antigua and during that time Annie fell into a breakdown taking the form of complete lassitude. She stayed in bed and watched as the room and the house became distorted. The British doctor could find nothing wrong with her except that she was rundown. Annie's problem is clearly psychological. She feels that her parents have stripped her of any identity, and she has sunk into confusion in order to try to save a precarious sense of self. This is symbolised in her erasure of all of the people in the family pictures, even herself, except for the shoes that she had bought despite her mother's protests (p. 120). Finally, Ma Chess appears one day when the steamer was not due and brings with her a knowledge of obeah, something the British doctor could not understand. Ma Chess had fought her own battle when her son John died. When he was sick, Ma Chess was sure that a western medical doctor was the last thing he needed; Pa Chess was sure that this was the one thing he did need. The old man had his way, and his son died. After her arrival in Antigua, the grand-mother settled on the floor at the foot of Annie's bed, eating and sleeping there, so that Annie was soon able to count on her. Ma Chess is the positive woman Annie has sought. The grandmother shows Annie the importance of her life and is willing to eat and sleep in the same room and even share the same bed with her, something her mother seemed unable to do since the girl was now sexually mature and a covert threat. Annie recovers immediately and thinks of leaving. It is significant that it is not the British medicine that made Annie well but the old ways of obeah.

After enduring a type of psychic death, the experience that Annie had so feared, she is ready to leave her family. The first words that come to her on the day she leaves are, 'My name is Annie John' (p. 130), signifying that she has recovered her identity, although only as distinct from other family members. Since Annie has survived psychic death, she can now suffer the separation that was the symbol of it. She realises that her father is 35 years older than her mother, and that he is now an old man, with some children older than his wife: 'I plan not only never to marry an old man but certainly never to marry at all' (p. 132). She sees perhaps why her mother could no longer be her first love after she had married a man so much older than herself, a teenager while he was middle-aged. On the walk to the jetty Annie remembers the first time her mother had sent her to the store alone: 'If I had just conquered Persia, she couldn't have been more proud of me' (p. 140). She sees this as a cruel betrayal, the first of many lessons on how to leave home. The only place she feels real pity about leaving is the library, the place where she learned to love words. Yet her mother's last words to her are prophetic: "'It doesn't matter what you do or where you go, I'll always be your mother and this will always be your home'" (p. 147). The novel tells the sad story of the woman in exile who feels that dreams of leaving are not as sweet as the time of loving, and that the mother country is never as welcoming as the mother.

ALISON DONNELL

She Ties Her Tongue: The Problems of Cultural Paralysis in Postcolonial Criticism

While the inception of postcolonial criticism marked a liberating rejection of the self-fulfilling criteria of a Eurocentric, patriarchal canon, if we now reflect with a critical eye on the effects of increasing centrality and popularity (albeit in the name of difference and marginality) within this growing discipline, its own orthodoxies and prejudices demand attention. Although postcolonial scholarship developed in opposition to prescriptive modes of thought, the consolidation and institutionalization of its works would seem to have generated in some respects an unhelpful homogenization of political intent and a stifling consensus of "good" practice. It might not be an exaggeration to suggest that postcolonialism has unwittingly become its own nemesis. Does not the imperative to celebrate, alongside the "political untouchability" and the terrorism of cultural sensitivity, generate a spectre of the "model," acceptable postcolonial response, which both chokes critics and arrests the possibilities for making meanings? The relentlessly positive reception afforded resistant subjects and rebellious discourses, the canonization of contemporary postcolonial women (writers), and the general academic conscience-pricking that have dominated postcolonial studies may have functioned (and continue to function) as important gestures against a profile of self-satisfied and defensive Eurocentric thought, but I would argue that they have a limited, if not an exhausted,

From *ARIEL*, January 1995. © 1992 by Alison Donnell.

value for those working within, rather than against, the field of postcolonial criticism and theory.

If postcolonialism's battle for intellectual and institutional recognition
has a record of successful campaigns, it also has its casualties. In its venture
to give voice to the silenced, little consideration was given to the fact that its
own vociferousness might be drowning out more subtle tones still striving to
be heard and still marginalized by the demands of academic recognition and
the attendant search for a politically flawless portfolio. It is perhaps not difficult to locate the politics of this dominant postcolonialism when we consider
that among these less-defined cadences are Creole and settler writings, those
early twentieth-century writings that often rest uncomfortably on the cusp of
coloniality, and writings that elect to work with rather than against European
models. Again, such an emphasis was significant to the project of redressing
the political and cultural biases of colonial discourse, but the persistent fore-
grounding of unproblematically postcolonial texts is not without consequences. Indeed, it is rather ironic that it is certain contemporary
postcolonial scholarship, with its labouring of voicelessness and absence, that
has served to license the neglect of some of its most fascinating (early)
archives and voices, which ostensibly failed to fulfil anti-imperialist agendas.
An example of this can be found in the common perception that postcolonial
women's writing only emerged in the 1970s and 1980s, a misapprehension
that reflects both a particular definition of *bona fide* postcoloniality and the
prominence given to contemporary and metropolitan texts.

In current postcolonial scholarship, nearly all critical attention
remains focused on those writers and works that show an obvious disen-
gagement from colonial culture, either through a geographical distance
(writings of exile and migration being particularly popular) or through a
historical one. Writings that are distanced from colonialism in this way
often offer models of identity formation and of aesthetic innovation that
can be identified as emerging either "after" or "outside" colonial paradigms. In other words, they are more comfortably "post" than they are
colonial. Perhaps most crucially for the future of the discipline, this preference for perfect political credentials alongside the propensity to deal in
perpetual marginality and voicelessness not only condemns writers to
dismal and oppressed self-defining narratives but burdens readers with a
baggage of unresolved cultural sensitivities, and critics with a tireless round
of congratulations and careful critiques.

It is my contention that a field of inquiry that could continue helpfully
and excitingly to be unsettling to intellectual and academic orthodoxies is in
danger of being settled prematurely by wider political imperatives, institutional pressures, and an entrenched cultural protocol. At the heart of this

issue lie the questions concerning who is allowed to speak and what manner of voice is permitted. Using Jamaica Kincaid's *A Small Place* as my textual locale, I am concerned with exploring some of the issues at stake in current postcolonial criticism and in particular the problem of cultural paralysis, which, I suggest, is a major political and intellectual impasse currently facing the discipline. My aim is not to admonish readers to suffer more anxiety, nor to have more confidence when reading postcolonial texts, neither is it to attack celebratory readings or to encourage more critical ones, but rather to think through the implications and consequences of these responses.

Too often, anxieties about approaching texts with a sensitive cultural valency can function as yet another reason for scholars to license their neglect, as Gayatri Chakravorty Spivak so neatly points out:

> The sort of breast-beating which stops the possibility of social change is to say, "I'm only a white male and cannot speak as a feminist," or, "I'm only a white male, I cannot speak for the blacks." . . . What we are asking for is that the hegemonic discourses, the holders of hegemonic discourse should de-hege-monize their position of the other rather than simply say, "O.K., sorry, we are just very good white people, therefore we do not speak for the blacks." That's the kind of breast-beating that is left behind at the threshold and then business goes on as usual. (121)

However, "de-hegemonization" can be a tricky process, and the study of postcolonial literatures clearly should foreground questions about positions (theoretical, ideological) and about the legitimacy of readings if it is to achieve this end. It is important to acknowledge that for readers whose study of postcolonial literatures involves readings across cultures and especially across the ex-colonial/postcolonial divide, questions concerning the right to read are highly charged.

It might be easy to respond to the proposition that "we" (British/Euro-pean/Western/white readers) should only study our "own" literature with the line about shutting down the French and German departments and closing all options on the eighteenth century. Indeed, there may be some sense to this line of argument, but it does not work so freely within the context of postcolonial cultures, where colonial history and the attendant schooling in European literature and literary criticism have been exercises in intellectual brutality. Indeed, the withdrawal and apprehension of cross-cultural readers often emerges not from their uncomfortable awareness of this legacy but from their inability to respond productively to it. The notion that "we" should limit inquiries to "our own" literature so often betrays a fear of confronting the questions "what is our own?" and, even more crucially, "who constitutes this 'we'?" It is perhaps with this challenging concentration on our own positions as readers that we should begin, not paralysed by insecurities concerning inappropriate knowledge and fears of misreadings but aware of and excited by the persistent uncertainty regarding acceptable ways to read and permissible theoretical parameters. To this end we must register the effects of placing power and responsibility along the writer/text/reader dynamic.

In his article "Constitutive Graphonomy: A Postcolonial Theory of Literary Writing," W. D. Ashcroft has suggested that "the political impetus of postcolonial theory has been to focus meaning at the site of production" (59). Indeed, beyond an analysis of resistance and counter-culture that might engender this focus, it would appear that those involved in postcolonial studies often prioritize the point of production because of their unwilling-ness to condone the "death of the author" as possessor of textual "truths." The tendency to give authority over to the writer's (cultural or political) intentions or to those readings produced by "native" critics signifies that postcolonial (and more acutely cross-cultural) readers are unsure about the availability of meaning within these texts and only feel comfortable with meanings that are culturally determined from the "inside." Certainly, the freedom to read and the continuum of meaning are more troubling concepts with reference to postcolonial texts and become more highly charged against a backdrop of cultural imperialism. Nevertheless, while a reluctance to embrace the "freedom" of meaning within postcolonial studies may result in a positive questioning of poststructuralism's sometimes-apolitical tendencies, it can also function as an intellectual shortcut that bypasses the issues of referential insecurity and ideological bias in its search for the culturally legit-imate meaning.

Clearly there is a value to "insider" readings, which might well offer insights not available to cross-cultural readers, but should they be valued as better, as equal, or simply as different from those that "outside" readers might produce? While meaning may well be culturally determined, surely it is not determined according to fixed or stable cultural positions. When we attempt to authenticate a writing or reading by virtue of its cultural orientation, we immediately fix that culture in a way that is unhelpful and betrays the very nature of cultural complexity within postcolonial societies, which we are at odds to point out elsewhere. Moreover, we take the "authentic" reading to represent certain cultural norms without fully accounting for the personal, educational, and institutional experience of each critic or writer in particular. In other words, when we attempt to stabilize culturally or fix the processes of signification (through reference to primary or secondary voices) are we not reverting to some kind of essentialism that we are usually so keen to condemn?

The problems of placing the "power to tell" in the hands of the writer or "native critic" are not only associated with the exclusivity of meaning that can emerge but are also related to the way in which we are simplifying our understanding of cultural forms in order to license a degree of validity and security that an "outside" reader can grasp. By weighting the culturally "safe" participant as the focus for attention, the cross-cultural reader is simplifying the locus of meaning and thereby reducing the complexity of the text and her or his own engagement with it.

However, the advent of the self-conscious reader within postcolonial studies can also be problematic. If one of the most vexed questions for the cross-cultural reader to address is "How do I avoid accusations of assumed universalism or appropriation?," one of the most popular strategies is to "bare all" and to identify an individual position, and its limitations, before commencing any analysis. Yet I have problems with the strategic preface, "As a white European feminist. . . ." After all, I am not really confident that this is what I am, or at least what I always am, or that even if I decided that it was what I was just now, whether I could maintain such a stable mode of identification through the course of a single piece of writing, or that even if I did, whether my readers would share any consensus on a term such as "feminist." Attempts to fix a participant in the act of cross-cultural communication is somehow to avoid the real questions concerning the negotiation of meaning that such an act should provoke. Although it is evidently important for readers to be self-conscious, as the apparently neutral or absent reader may well be the naive and undiscriminating Eurocentric reader, the "As a . . ." strategy can become habitual, unthinking, and thus "meaningless." Moreover, a disclaimer can operate paradoxically as a way of claiming all the power in achieving meaning for the reader and of thus erasing issues of cultural difference altogether. A declaration of limits can actually work as a legitimation device, suggesting that any reading (rather than many readings) is "equally valid" without consideration being given to the possibilities of multiple or contested meanings. It would appear, then, that an awareness of the various positions of reader and writer can be helpful and interesting, but that such awareness should not be reduced to competition, with readings of postcolonial texts developing into a bidding system in which cultural and ideological credentials are listed as the markers for deciding who can claim the most "authentic" ownership of meaning.

If some of the dilemmas associated with cultural paralysis can be traced to this preoccupation with the credentials for the postcolonial text and critic, then a little book called *A Small Place*, which has puzzled, infuriated, and fiercely engaged everyone I know who has read it, provides an interesting (counter) discourse on postcolonial cultural protocol. As I hope to demonstrate, this text manages to press the panic buttons of various cultural positions and to utilize irony—a particularly slippery if not subjective trope—in order to pose effectively questions concerning the right to speak for and to speak of, and the consequences of these practices in terms of the politics of postcolonialism.

It might be helpful to begin by considering why it is that of all Jamaica Kincaid's works, *A Small Place* has received the least critical attention. The generic definition of this text clearly has been crucial to its reception—it has been published variously as autobiography, politics, history, sociology (but not, as far as I know, as fiction); such reading strategies, which emphasize the factual and historical content, predetermine the status and particular purchase granted to the narrative voice. Indeed, on a first reading, it is not difficult to appreciate why this text has been described as "uncompromising," as an "incontestable denunciation," and is commonly read transparently as a tirade against the colonial legacy and the neo-colonial tourist industry (Ferguson 131–38). In its simplest guise, *A Small Place* is a most ungenerous reconstruction of the tourist's-eye-view of Antigua and a simultaneous commentary on the ruinous effects of colonial and postcolonial projects on the island; the second reading powerfully realigns the vision of the first. However, while in one sense this text is pure polemic—a strident and lucid denunciation of tourism and the comforting belief that colonialism is "post"—just under the straightforward indignation of the narrative voice, which claims with confidence to identify criminal from victim, and right from wrong, lies an indeterminacy of meaning, crucially linked to the undecidability about where this voice is speaking from, and for whom.

Following on from Giovanna Covi, who has provided an insightful analysis of the aesthetic strategies of this text, drawing attention to the "faked, primitive child-like voice" (94) and to what lies "under the pretended naivete of the speaking voice" (94), I wish to explore the politics and the ethics of *A Small Place*. I want to suggest that one way to reveal "what lies beneath" is to read *A Small Place* as a consummate work of ventriloquism that deploys a whole series of voices in order to debate the values and limitations of the cultural discourses and positions associated with postcolonialism. In order to present some evidence for this reading, I wish to call on Nicholas Thomas's engaging and careful "anthropological" work, *Colonialism's Culture*, and in particular on Thomas's analysis of colonialism as "a cultural process; its discoveries and trespasses are imagined and energized through signs, metaphors and narratives; even what would seem its purest moments of profit and violence have been mediated and enframed by structures of meaning."

To my mind, Kincaid displays a keen awareness of the way in which the culture of colonialism (in Thomas's terms) persisted, as discursive structures were inherited alongside the more visible institutional power structures. In this way, *A Small Place* not only explores the continuity of corrupt political and economic practice in Antigua after Independence but more crucially plays on and with the cultural practices of writing and reading that are complicit to such perpetuation. Kincaid re-enters this culture, rehearsing its rhetoric and idioms to produce a multi-accentuated text that is both a direct political statement on neo-colonialism and an ironic commentary on the politics of postcolonialism—the two operating simultaneously.

Although the irony of the piece is subtly sustained, it is explosive to its meaning and transforms the text from a monologic attack on the tourist by the "native" into a disturbing series of cultural observations directed at a range of targets. As Linda Hutcheon has explored in "Circling the Down-spout of Empire," irony often functions as a key subversive trope within postcolonial criticism. However, in *A Small Place*, one of the discourses that Kincaid is "working within . . . and contesting at the same time" (Hutcheon 171) is that of postcolonialism itself.

The text's most immediate irony is achieved by the narrator's "trying on" of the colonial tongue, which glibly appropriates its object of study. From the very beginning, this text parades an astonishingly arrogant propensity to speak for others, as the narrator assumes the right to speak for the tourist: "If you go to Antigua as a tourist, this is what you will see" (3). More-over, this assured voice (which masquerades as innocent) assumes all visitors, indeed all readers, to be tourists and cultural voyeurs of a kind, by impli-cating "you," the reader, within "you," the tourist. This adoption of colonial discourse's unproblematic "speaking for" forces the postcolonial reader to experience the process of being constructed, unfixing her or his desired posi-tion as reconstructed reader. Yet the irony latent in this voice makes any attempt to fix its moral orientation impossible, and the text's drive towards destabilizing positions becomes clearer as Kincaid unfixes her own position with the same ironic tone. During the persuasive and sardonic account of the tourist's myopic vision that opens the text, the narrator suddenly turns with "[t]hey [the Antiguans] do not like you. *They do not like me!*" (17). Although this second formulation functions as an absent echo in the tourist's mind, it is also a record of the irony inherent in Kincaid's vituperative attack on tourists, as she herself catches sight of the island from the plane window, a tourist of sorts, having left Antigua at the age of 17.

Probably the most sensitive and hostile of Kincaid's works, *A Small Place* refuses its own soft target of the tourist in favour of a range of more contentious offenders. This is not to suggest that the book shies away from a condemnation of tourism, but rather that it probes more thoroughly and painfully the question of responsibility for postcolonial failures (economic, social, and psychological). As Helen Tiffin has pointed out, *A Small Place* is a "direct address to Americans, English (or worse, Europeans)" (36), but it is not just a word in the ears of those who go in search of sunshine and exotica; it is also an address to those paralysed by liberal guilt. This passage, for example, explicitly addresses the implied reader/cultural voyeur: "Have you ever wondered why it is that all we seem to have learned from you is how to corrupt our societies and how to be tyrants? You will have to accept that this is mostly your fault" (35). Surely the narrative voice here presents an exaggerated version, almost a pastiche, of the postcolonial text that plays upon white readers' *Angst*. Moreover, the immediacy and tenacity of the response to this cultural trigger would seem to disclose the acute anxiety, if not critical paralysis, on the part of the cross-cultural reader, who would accept willingly her or his assigned position as oppressor and not dare to read such a statement as ironic or provocative.

By planting such an extreme version of the manifesto guiding certain postcolonial texts, Kincaid is able to disclose the way in which meaning is paralysed by cultural censorship. Frozen in a moment of guilt, "outside" critics of postcolonial literatures are too often prevented from asking themselves "what is the value of this text?" because they are so obsessed with the dilemma of whether they have the right to ask that question, or are so assured by its ability to uncover their liberal guilt that they need not question its value further. Equally, this statement is a means to scrutinize the credentials and value of those postcolonial texts that rely on their readers' guilt. By presenting the guiding motivation of these texts in such crude terms, the narrator lays bare a political position that has been both significant and successful in the battle to rewrite the script of colonial encounter in order to provoke a reconsideration of the merits of this strategy.

It is through this unveiling and opening of the seams with which postcolonialism has sought to join writers and readers, ex-colonized and ex-colonizers, that *A Small Place* bids for a thorough consideration of how all groups might now ethically and effectively respond to each other. By dislocating the agendas to which many postcolonial readers and writers have subscribed, in addition to the more obvious misapprehensions of the tourist's version of cross-cultural encounter, Kincaid's text draws attention to the ways in which political paralysis might have become the unwitting bedfellow of political untouchability, and thus forces a consideration of how within postcolonial situations (both textual and political) cultural analysis and interaction can be achieved helpfully.

However, if *A Small Place* refuses the easy option in terms of "speaking against" by constantly extending its range of targets, then it is equally uneasy about "speaking for" and offering an insider, legitimate, unambiguous meaning. Indeed, it seems to me that Kincaid is most fierce in her address to the Antiguan people, whom she censures for failing to accept responsibility and to engage critically with their present situation. It is interesting that in one interview Kincaid confidently declared, "[t]he thing that I am branded with and the thing that I am denounced for, I claim as my own. I am illegitimate, I am ambiguous" ("Interview" 129); she has been widely chastised for daring to write in such an ambivalent fashion about this "small place," her birthplace, Antigua, while living in the distant and more affluent Maine, USA. The ambiguity of her own cultural location, to which she draws attention in this text, fuels the debate over the value of her text—her perceived betrayal of her "cultural home" itself betraying the expectation of the postcolonial writer's duty to speak for her or his community. It is not an expectation that Kincaid is willing to fulfil, as she writes in *A Small Place*:

> In a small place, people cultivate small events. The small event is isolated, blown up, turned over and over, and then absorbed into the everyday, so that at any moment it can and will roll off the inhabitants of the small place's tongues. For the people in a small place, every event is a domestic event; the people in a small place cannot see themselves in a larger picture, they cannot see that they may be part of a chain of something, anything. (52–53)

This "small place-small mind" equivalence becomes almost a refrain during the second half of the text, reflecting on a mindset that is also frozen in a particular mode of response and cannot free itself from colonial paradigms.

After a sustained commentary on the linguistic, geographical, and moral imposition of the English during Antigua's period of colonial rule, the narrator declares her anguished but futile response to the phenomenon of cultural dispossession, still pertinent to the nominally "postcolonial" Antigua of the 1980s:

> Nothing can erase my rage—not an apology, not a large sum of money, not the death of the criminal—for this wrong can never be made right, and only the impossible can make me still: can a way be found to make what happened not have happened? And so look at this prolonged visit to the bile duct that I am making, look at how bitter, how dyspeptic just to sit and think about these things makes me. (32)

Although exercising the right to speak from an angry and unreconstructed position is a significant and challenging aspect of this text, again the split signification that the ironic tongue enacts also allows an articulation of this position to function as a criticism. *A Small Place* highlights the problems of a postcolonial condition that simply involves a reiteration of external oppression, as this can operate as an excuse for those who wish to behave as neocolonialists on their own territory and also can effect an entrapment of consciousness that offers limiting conceptual and ontological possibilities. It is also, as I have suggested, critical of those who "trade off" this condition, including writers and readers of postcolonial texts.

By staging the problems of being culturally paralysed and questioning how ethical it is to position yourself as eternally, unalterably sinner or sinned upon within a colonial dialectic of oppressor/victim, *A Small Place* is pointing to an unhelpful reliance on fixed models of cultural experience and an entrapment within forms of analysis that ultimately deny the possibilities of different forms of cultural interaction. It would seem that troubling the beliefs and positions that comfort us (whether "we" be the myopic tourist, the arrogant colonizer, the oppressed ex-colonized, or the enlightened postcolonial reader) is the text's most consistent quality. By doing violence to certain modes of perception and discourse, the narrative cautions us that to be aware of wrongs and to apportion (or to accept) blame are not adequate responses but rather are markers of the limitations of certain liberal and nationalist projects that have failed to effect any change in the particular ways of positioning each other across ex-colonizer/ex-colonial divides.

Although *A Small Place* may issue an imperative for change through its aggressive dissatisfaction with entrenched modes of being in and of addressing this situation, it does not clear a new path forward or offer us new and better positions; rather, it dismantles the very moral and political divides that have helped postcolonial critics to advance their work. In contrast to the period of colonial rule during which, as Kincaid so succinctly points out, ethical divides were far clearer—"We felt superior, for we were so much better behaved and we were full of grace, and these people were so badly behaved and they were so completely empty of grace" (30)—the postcolonial period offers no such comforting moral ground. It is my suggestion that this text, which has managed to hit the sore points of both British and Antiguan readers, generates a significant level of agitation within its readers in order to make us aware of the inadequacies of postcolonial scholarship and of liberal and national politics, which very often retain the concentration on colonial paradigms and tend to consolidate the historical divisions between the powerful and the powerless, those generating discourse and those being inscribed by it, rather than seeking to dismantle them. The text's candid narration of colonial history makes it clear that we must not ignore what has happened, but its equally harsh rendition of the present as paralysing "political perfection" strongly suggests that neither must we rely on a reiteration or a confession of past wrongs (both moral and representational) as a way forward. However, if it does not provide us with alternatives to these impasses within the text, is it helpful in any way to those of us already uncomfortably aware of the problems inherent in postcolonial studies?

As *A Small Place* spirals towards a climax (a narrative movement effected by the constant turning to and turning on issues and peoples), one might anticipate a final conflict if reading the text simply as a polemic against neocolonialism. Yet the final statement is both a fusion and a radical disclosure of the interests of the text in process:

> Eventually, the masters left, in a kind of way; eventually, the slaves were freed, in a kind of way. The people in Antigua now, the people who really think of themselves as Antiguans (and the people who would immediately come to your mind when you think about what Antiguans might be like; I mean, supposing you were to think about it), are the descendants of those noble and exalted people, the slaves. Of course, *the whole thing is*, once you cease to be a master, once you throw off your master's yoke, you are no longer human rubbish, you are just a human being, and all the things that adds up to. So, too, with the slaves. Once they are no longer slaves, once they are free, they are no longer noble and exalted; they are just human beings. (80–81; emphasis added)

I would suggest that this final statement is an act of significant provocation that transforms the text's focus on discursive practice in order to demand a consideration of what lies beyond discourse. It functions as a will to participate, to react, to object, to be indignant, to take on the responsibility of freeing ourselves from these cultural dead-ends. It is in this way that *A Small Place* approaches some of the most vexing questions within literary criticism, and postcolonial literary criticism in particular—"where is the subject outside of discourse?" and "what is the possible relationship between discourse and agency, between postcolonial scholarship and postcolonial politics?"

It is perhaps through the ventriloquism of this text that we can locate one answer to these questions, as the ironic appropriation of another's voice allows the fracture between discourse and the speaking subject to be glimpsed and a possible point at which agency can begin to be identified. In this way, Kincaid's text reiterates the radical possibilities of mimicry, to which Henry Louis Gates, Jr. and Homi Bhabha have pointed, by providing a complex example of the way in which engaging in an other's discourse need not repeat the other's values nor assume the position assigned to you within that discourse. However, *A Small Place* also provides a more fundamental dismantling of cultural positions and projects and thus forces us to respond to the movement that is occurring, both literally and intellectually, in terms of definitions of cultural identity, and incites us to claim agency through these possibilities for change. One of the most important qualities of this text is the positive contingency of identity, which Stuart Hall identifies in his article "Cultural Identity and Diaspora":

> Cultural identity is a matter of "becoming" as well as of "being." It belongs to the future as much as to the past. It is not something which already exists, transcending place, time, history and culture. Cultural identities come from somewhere, have histories. But, like everything which is historical, they undergo constant transformation. Far from being eternally fixed in some essentialised past, they are subject to the continuous "play" of history, culture and power. (394)

Kincaid's evocative and effective blending of realism and optimism, of the imperative to expose neo-colonial projects and yet not to become entrapped or limited by them, does not deny the significance of historical dispossession, or the desire and the will to belong, but rather calls for a revaluation of historical narratives and cultural positionings.

My suggestion is that *A Small Place* does not just ask for an end to economic imperialism and the legitimation of feelings of anger and retribution (although clearly these are crucial functions of the text) but that its most urgent demand is for an end to entrenched modes of cultural positioning and for ground on which a postcolonial individual can be more than just a positioned subject or a subject position. In other words, it tries to be more than a discourse on a discourse and to disclose how postcolonial scholarship's concentration on identifying positioned subjects can often become more of an interest in discourse than in postcolonial subjects. It also draws attention to the way in which much postcolonial writing that has sought to react against assigned positions by inscribing the fullness of lives and subjectivities and the intricacies of the cultural codes of the formerly colonized merely has traded in the same limiting modes of representation and ideas of culturally authentic and stable identities. In this way, the text makes a demand on both a Western readership that wishes only to be reassured of its sensitivity to the oppression of others and its worthiness of mind as well as on the population of a small place, an ex-colonized society, which wishes to point ceaselessly to the evils of colonization as the *raison d'être* of all of its problems and misjudgements, to widen their fields of vision and perceive the constraints of consolidating and concentrating on only their own positions.

Perhaps most importantly, *A Small Place* issues a powerful reminder that the very attraction of this area of study is that issues are highly charged and that the problems and the texts that we address have a significance beyond intellectual amusement. It is perhaps only by daring to look beyond the politics of the academy and the constraints of "correctness" that we have constructed for ourselves that we can avoid being petrified by the difficult moral and political questions that postcolonial studies can and should pose. Kincaid's text may well be a prolonged meditation on tourism, but it most powerfully articulates the need for postcolonial subjects, readers and writers, to be open to a mobility, and a journeying, that is the very antithesis of tourism, which involves intellectual, even emotional, movement, negotiation, and relocation. Although such a journey may appear hazardous to our intellectual comfort and our political well-being, it may offer a way out of paralysis and towards more ethical, interesting, and empowering possibilities for the definition of both self and other.

MOIRA FERGUSON

Lucy *and the Mark of the Colonizer*

As I go on writing, I feel less and less interested in the approval of the First World, and I never had the approval of the world I came from, so now I don't know where I am. I've exiled myself yet again.
—Donna Perry, "An Interview with Jamaica Kincaid."

"But I couldn't speak, so I couldn't tell her that my mother was my mother and that society and history and culture and other women in general were something else altogether."
—*Lucy*

[The third scenario] is the scene where this new thing [cultural positionality] is worked out, and the difficulty we are having is the difficulty of that discourse emerging.
—Stuart Hall, "Third Scenario: Theory and Politics of Location."

In her first post-Antiguan novel, *Lucy* (1990), whose title character travels from Antigua to the United States, Jamaica Kincaid continues a fictional/semi-autobiographical saga that was initiated in earlier texts, *Annie John* and *A Small Place*. In a limited way, these texts "acquire mass, density, and referential power among themselves and thereafter in the culture at

From *Modern Fiction Studies*, Summer 1993. © 1993 by Moira Ferguson.

large"; they constitute a "strategic formation," constructing themselves as counterdiscourse to the dominant culture (*Orientalism* 20). As an African-Caribbean writer, that is, Kincaid speaks to and from the position of the other. Not only does she specify confrontations along class/race/gender axes, she also unmasks "the results of those distortions internalized within our consciousness of ourselves and one another" (Lorde 147).

In *Lucy*, Kincaid pursues these confrontations via diverse strategies. Casting aside adolescence, *Lucy* tells her own story while doubling as a representative of black Antiguans; a willing recorder of the island's oral narrative, she rescripts familiar thematics as well as exploring new ones. For example, *Lucy* takes place in Manhattan during the 1960s just prior to Antigua's attainment of partial independence from Britain in 1967, contributing another layer to a collective *bildungsroman* that reverts back in time to the end of *Annie John* when seventeen-year old Annie sails for Britain. The protagonists of the two novels, while differently named, are similar in their Caribbean sensibilities and their commitment to unmasking hypocrisy. Gender is a paramount issue in both novels, with the image of the mother-child dyad extending in *Lucy* to a colonizing motherland as well as a biological maternality. Across these two novels, then, sexual politics are seen as integral to the colonial and postcolonial imperative.

The narrator of *Lucy* is a twenty-year-old black Antiguan female who craves control of her life. She takes a job as an au pair in New York as part of her move toward independence. From the day she arrives in New York from the Caribbean and retires to bed to avoid further overload, she is determined to be an agent rather than a passive receiver. Unlike the protagonists of other texts, she is surrounded almost exclusively by white people, not only in her immediate household but also within her circle of friends.

As an expatriate residing in the United States and occupying diverse subject positions, Lucy has to cope with strategies aimed at colonizing her as a British "subject." She has to negotiate her way through differing representations of power, first with the husband, Lewis, a middle-aged lawyer, and second with his wife, Mariah, a rich but emotionally dominated and somewhat naive Anglo-Saxon woman from a distinguished Michigan family who initially thinks the world lies at her feet. Worth noting, too, is the fact that Kincaid in a telling reversal of the erasure of African names uses no patronymic for Lewis and Mariah: in this way "the family" of the novel is discursively and deliberately homogenized.

As an indictment of the colonizing project, *Lucy* is comparable to *A Small Place*. In the latter, the narrator argues that people in a postcolonial situation tend to act as an oppressed population. They have little sense of the past, present, and future and treat everything on an *ad hoc* basis. This ahistorical attitude corrupts people by dissolving or eliminating class divisions and the capacity to analyze those differences. Alive to nuance, changing moods, and events, Lucy adopts a more explicitly counter-hegemonic stance after biding her time in a postcolonial setting. She grounds whatever she sees in an alternative vision that resists the domination of the colonial setting.

Thus, despite one reviewer's complaints that Jamaica Kincaid "dissociates herself from blacks" in her fiction, Lucy's cultural awareness is abundantly evident (Adisa 6). She employs a strategy of cultural reversal, revealing how the political legatees of residual colonial culture live their lives and think about their cultural positionality. In *Lucy*, Kincaid thematizes hegemonic treatment of those regarded as native "others." Lucy is simultaneously fetishized and condescended to in a revamped form of old hierarchical relations existing between the colonizer and the colonized as her employers and their friends try to homogenize difference and subsume it within their jurisdiction. They do so by pretending that the power dynamic between the "haves" and the "have nots" does not dominate everyday life.

The maid in Lewis and Mariah's house is more candid, though no more empowered than is Lucy by her recognition of race/class differences in this domestic realm. Attuned to an intra-class pecking order, she tries to make Lucy feel stupid and worthless, charging her with speaking as if she were calcified:

> She said that I spoke like a nun, I walked like one also, and that everything about me was so pious that it made her feel at once sick to her stomach and sick with pity just to look at me. And so, perhaps giving way to the latter feeling, she said that we should dance, even though she was quite sure I didn't know how. (11)

In response to this criticism, Lucy displays pride in her origins: while an album sung by three insincere but "beautiful" white singers is played, Lucy energetically sings a calypso "about a girl who ran away to Port-of-Spain, Trinidad, and had a good time, with no regrets" (12). In the face of racist stereotypes, she claims herself and her history. She may occupy the maid's room—"a box in which cargo traveling a long way should be shipped" as she describes it—but tellingly adds: "I was not cargo" (7). From the beginning, consciously or not, Lucy sets out to undermine metropolitan authority and asserts her right to contest it.

Yet Lucy's relation to "origins" is more ambiguous than her singing indicates. In the portrayal of Mariah, one can see reflected Lucy's continuing altercation—albeit more muted than in *Annie John*—with her biological mother. The sequence in which Mariah is represented begins with her reaction to the weather, continues with an incident in which daffodils are projected as a trope of colonialism, and concludes with Lucy's indignity at her mother's scolding about the dangers of the New York underground. Mariah's excitement at the weather and the sight of daffodils perplexes Lucy: "How do you get to be that way?" she wonders (*Lucy* 20). She cannot fathom how a windy day can make one person more agitated than someone facing, say, a daily drought. What causes such priorities? Is it simply that some lives are lived at a trivialized, even perilously self-indulgent level? Could it be guilt or compensation? Later when the paper-thin surface of Mariah's life cracks, Lucy implicitly receives her answers.

Kincaid tellingly scatters yellow images throughout the two incidents concerning the notorious daffodils. Yellow, in these passages, represents domination and the facade of beauty that masks decay in a mirage of power. Mariah is one of the "six yellow-haired heads of various sizes [that] were bunched as if they were a bouquet of flowers tied together by an unseen string" (12). Members of the family, from the point of view of colonized people, are indistinguishable; they live in a kitchen in different shades of (jaundiced?) yellow where Mariah "with her pale-yellow skin and yellow hair, stood still in this almost celestial light, and she looked glossed, no blemish or mark of any kind on her cheek or anywhere else" (27). Mariah's scatheless, euroidealized face contrasts sharply in two later incidents with two scarred faces and a potentially scarred one: of Lucy's mother, her friend, and Lucy herself. The friend bears a scar on her right cheek from a human bite after a quarrel with another woman over a man (24) while the face of Lucy's mother has been gashed by a monkey (54). Lucy herself states that she will "end up with a mark somewhere" (25). African-Caribbean women, Lucy postulates, cannot remain artificially faultless.

The second appearance of the daffodils involves Mariah's insistence that Lucy look at daffodils after Lucy carefully explains why she loathes the flowers. Mariah brushes off Lucy's angry monologue about being forced to recite William Wordsworth's poem "The Daffodils" when she was growing up—stark evidence of residual British culture. Mariah's response is culpably naive:

> I told it to her with such an amount of anger . . . Mariah reached out to me and, rubbing her hand against my cheek, said, "What a history you have." I thought there was a little bit of envy [note Lucy spots no condescension] in her voice, and I said, "You are welcome to it if you like." (18–19)

As a predictably ethnocentric employer, Mariah forces Lucy's gaze on the daffodils through trickery, just as Lucy was forced to recite the poem:

"[She] took me to a garden, a place she described as among her favorites in the world. She covered my eyes with a handkerchief, and then, holding me by the hand, she walked me to a spot in a clearing" (28). Lucy then is forced to gaze on the very daffodils themselves. To this form of cultural intimidation, Lucy responds violently: "I wanted to kill them. I wished that I had an enormous scythe; I would just walk down the path, dragging it alongside me, and I would cut these flowers down at the place where they emerged from the ground" (29). Mariah cannot comprehend Lucy's response: "Her eyes sank back in her head as if they were protecting themselves, as if they were taking a rest after some unexpected hard work. It wasn't her fault. It wasn't my fault. But nothing could change the fact that where she saw beautiful flowers I saw sorrow and bitterness" (30).

The fact that William Wordsworth wrote several "Lucy" poems raises the question of Kincaid's possible ironies. Although we learn later—a point I shall return to—that Lucy is named after Lucifer himself, Wordsworth's Lucy and Kincaid's Lucy are also mirror-like; one mimics the other. "In Strange Fits of Passion Have I Known," Wordsworth's Lucy is continually gazed at by her lover who fears that Lucy "should be dead," his emotion not dissimilar to Lucy's longing for her own mother's death later in the novel. In the second Lucy poem, "She Dealt through the Untrodden Ways," the speaker's grief at someone unnamed who lived alone once again resonates with countless unnamed colonized daughters of empire who die unsung. Dying unsung is something Kincaid's Lucy is determined will not happen to her. In "Three Years She Grew," a personified Nature decides to construct Lucy, only to be thwarted by her death. Similarly, Kincaid's Lucy cannot successfully be molded by the colonial system commonly configured as "natural" human progress. Lucy's alliance to nature, implicit in the popular conception of indigenous people, is rescripted in the fourth Lucy poem, "A Slumber Did My Spirit Steal," where Lucy eternally circles "with rocks, and stones, and trees."

But the fifth and last Lucy poem is the clinching one. In "I Traveled Among Unknown Men," a patriot narrates how he cherishes the image of Lucy in a cottage turning her wheel and contemplating green fields as she expires. The very idea of Kincaid's Lucy coming from a drought-ridden, arid Antigua and constructing a garment from the cotton threads of empire while gazing on lush well-watered English pastures is ludicrous, a mockery of empire in general and Wordsworth specifically as a preeminent cultural icon.

Mariah's earlier envying of Lucy's history—the remarkable envy of the oppressor toward the oppressed—receives a face in a later incident when Mariah claims her kinship with Lucy, presumably in an effort to receive absolution. She craves to identify with oppression so much that she boasts about her "Indian blood" (40). Lucy does not disguise her contempt: "Why claim a thing like that? I myself had Indian blood in me. My grandmother is a Carib Indian. That makes me one-quarter Carib Indian" (40). She mulls over the implications of Mariah's assertion: "Underneath everything I could swear she says it as if she were announcing her possession of a trophy" (40). Mariah desires forgiveness for colonial complicity, but Lucy cannot function so glibly, nor can she countenance Mariah's efforts to rewrite history. In her attempts to rub out the past and resite Lucy, Mariah contributes to the conventional totalizing narrative of old colonial and new postcolonial relations. With pointed words that cut through the malaise she feels Mariah is (unconsciously) spreading, Lucy inquires sarcastically: "How do you get to be the sort of victor who can claim to be the vanquished also?" (41). Lucy has trouble coming to terms with people who trivialize life-and-death matters; in her eyes, they live superficial lives. Her assessment of Mariah temporarily enables her to nurture a pyrrhic victory: "It was hollow, my triumph, I could feel that. But I held on to it just the same" (41). Her elation is empty because she cannot separate her growing affection for Mariah—who is often imaged as Lucy's biological mother—from her growing distaste for Mariah's understated, reactionary views.

Lucy's contradictory feelings echo something Jamaica Kincaid said in an interview: "I feel that, in particular, my own history is much about dominion; in fact we were called 'the dominion,' and all the colonies were 'the dominions'" (Perry 501). In the novel, Lucy's initial disgust at the imperial expropriation of colonized culture by that of the colonizer is gradually displaced on to the daffodils which come to represent the "past" and "present" of her life. After the initially painful incident with the daffodils, Mariah (as if to underscore her colonial credentials and power under the guise of benevolence) informs Lucy of her plans. En route to Michigan she wants Lucy to share one of her favorite experiences: "spending the night on a train and waking up to breakfast on the train as it moved through freshly plowed fields" (28). The significance of the daffodils and the plowed fields that gesture toward plantation slavery is not lost on Mariah. However, when that sight finally comes into view, Lucy veils her powerful reactions—she experiences a moment of insight as if to say that the boss must not know what the insurrectionary is thinking:

> Early that morning, Mariah left her own compartment to come and tell that we were passing through some of those freshly plowed fields she loved so much. She drew up my blind, and when I saw mile after mile of turned-up earth, I said, a cruel tone to my voice, "Well, thank God I didn't have to do that." I don't know if she understood what I meant, for in that statement I meant many different things. (33)

The vision of ploughed fields illuminates another trope of colonialism just as it represents Mariah's denial of Lucy's African Caribbean heritage and the power of Lucy's historical memory. Once again, Mariah's blithe ethnocentric attitudes enable her to find joy in something that marks atrocity for Lucy's ancestors. In her (culpable) naiveté, Mariah recalls the tourist in *A Small Place*, but in this instance Lucy silently registers the dimensions of Mariah's ignorance. In the dining car, the diners resemble Mariah's relatives, while the people waiting on the family strike Lucy as resembling herself. On closer inspection, Lucy decides the employees are less familiar and more supine than she at first thought: "My relatives always gave backchat" (32). Mariah's telling obliviousness to this racist scenario sharply contrasts with Lucy's perplexed outrage:

> Mariah did not seem to notice what she had in common with the other diners, or what I had in common with the waiters. She acted in her usual way, which was that the world was round and we all agreed on that, when I knew that the world was flat and if I went to the edge I would fall off. (32)

The text exposes the anti-colonial fury that had earlier so bewildered Mariah. Once at Lake Michigan, Mariah excitedly draws Lewis and the children into her holiday projects:

> She said, "Taa-daah! Trout!" and made a big sweep with her hands, holding the fish up in the light, so that rainbowlike colors shone on their scales. She sang out, "I will make you fishers of men," and danced around me. After she stopped, she said, "Aren't they beautiful? Gus and I went out in my old boat—my very, very old boat—and we caught them. My fish. This is supper. Let's go feed the minions." (37).

The word "minions" reminds Lucy of her condition as an Antiguan in an Anglo household: "A word like that would haunt someone like me, the place where I came from was a dominion of someplace else" (37). A further unpacking of the word "minions" also recalls San Domingo where the most successful anti-slavery revolution took place in 1791. Inspired by the trout scene with its fusion of fish and minions, Lucy tells Mariah a quaint childhood tale about eagerly asking her mother how the fishes were cooked during the miracle of the loaves and fishes. This complex imbrication of imperial culture and Mariah's pointed boast of her Christian leadership role—"I will make you fishers of men"—elicits from Lucy a response similar to the one she tendered to the family maid. She cancels out Mariah's subtle claiming of a missionary role with a story about too little food for the people—a notorious fact of colonial life. Lucy knows that Mariah remains clueless about the implications of growing up in a British "dominion," a code word and not-so-subtle euphemism for hegemony over land-peasant ancestors (Cudjoe 399). Although Lucy makes a point of underscoring cultural differences in this scene, Mariah still cannot comprehend that Lucy's experience of the world induces an oppositional understanding of "culture."

Intertwining sexuality, postcolonial recognitions, and gender relations, fish and fishermen resonate throughout Kincaid's texts. In this scene with Mariah, fishing bears multiple symbols; not only is it emblematic of Antiguan culture, but it implies a New Testament tropology involving the apostolic succession and Jesus' famous miracle. In making the comparison to her mother's preparation of fish, Lucy reverses again the metonymic chain: by scrutinizing the colonizing gain (chain) on the same subjects, she highlights the clandestine method deployed by colonizers to remake societies in their own image. Lucy exposes the suppressed rhetoric of the imperial system.

Mariah's underside is further exposed during an episode figuring another colonial reversal. Vanishing marshlands preoccupy the ecology-minded Mariah, symbolically as well as literally. Things are no longer what they used to be in her family or in her Michigan environment. Lucy laughs to herself at the self-delusory activity that prevents Mariah and women of her class from facing the global evils they helped to create and maintain. Mariah and her affluent friends can burn with anger at the destruction of the ecological system while Mariah employs someone whose people suffer drought and chronic deprivation all year round. Lucy only hints at the ricocheting ironies. Mariah's preoccupation with marshlands, with mud and viscosity, stresses her distance from moral purity.

The rape of the people as well as the land is an old colonial signifier. Now in one of its postcolonial transformations, these rapes hurt the colonizers themselves. Moreover, colonial agents do not recognize their own inconsistencies because they mystify the profit they take from the rape of the land, an evasion constitutive of a colonial mentality. Lewis and his class-allied peers buy stock and invest in corporations that cut down rain forests, turning natural acres into developed areas. For all Mariah knows, they could be buying timber and mining stock. Kincaid deftly inserts a question articulated by the child Louisa to suggest this complex of issues while the *mise en scène* simultaneously reinscribes Lucy's old negative relationship with her mother:

[Mariah] moaned against this vanishing idyll [when marshland flourished] so loudly that Louisa, who was just at the age where

if you are a girl you turn against your mother, "Well, what used
to be here before this house we are living in was built?" It was a
question I had wanted to ask, but I couldn't bear to see the hurt
such a question would bring to Mariah's face. (72)

Louisa's question reveals Mariah's complicity with metropolitan power just
as Kincaid's multiple protagonists charge their "mother" with complicity in
the law of the father. The child Louisa queries Mariah for her institutional
complicity just as Lucy—as well as Annie John—blame their mothers
personally for colonial corruption. Ironically, a dual maternality marks colo-
nial-patriarchal hegemony.

With no comprehension of context, Mariah yearns for days gone by.
She seems oblivious to their impact on Lucy and her formerly enslaved
ancestors. In the hands of the colonizer, environmental reform is just another
form of control. Acquiring a more discriminating knowledge of the present
has helped Lucy recover and understand her past. That knowledge has
subverted her positive fantasies about Mariah and Lewis. From this point on,
no one can drown out certain radical possibilities that she begins to envisage.
Inevitably and unwittingly, Lewis, Mariah, and their peers constitute themselves for Lucy in their own misrecognitions.

By the fourth chapter of the novel, "Cold Heart," the intertwining
issues of gender, colonialism, and ethnocentricity become more dramatically
apparent. In contrast to her employers' disintegrating marriage, Lucy initiates a process of self-healing as she pierces through white liberal sham. Early
on, as Lucy watches the entire family happily going out to dinner, she views
them as through an open window: "I was looking at ruins, and I knew it right
then. The actual fall of this Rome I hoped not to be around to see" (88).
Through such insights Lucy comes to terms with her own naiveté in
desiring—from the distance of Antigua—a situation whose exploitative and
deceptive nature becomes apparent up close. In recent interviews, Jamaica
Kincaid talks of the fatuity of the imperial history books that she devours.
The mention of Rome recalls the proscription of paganism (involved in how
people like Dinah regard Lucy), the riots of Thessalonica (incidents in which
islanders, formerly slaves, are expected to "misbehave"), and the invasion of
"territory" in the name of civilization. One irony of the metaphor recalling
early Roman invaders lies in the fact that the "vandals" (often a code name
for native peoples) Alaric and Gaiseric sacked Rome in 410 A.D. and 455
A.D. respectively. The metaphorical density in "the fall of this Rome," its
hybridity, encapsulates not only familial disintegration but its colonizing
aspect and Lucy's role as the outsider-servant who refuses at many levels to
mimic or participate in the system. "The Roman empire [Kincaid suggests]

fell because its social structure . . . was founded . . . on slavery" (Perowne xvii).

These complex allusions are compounded when Mariah encourages Lucy to study Paul Gauguin, the postimpressionist painter who was also a successful half-commission man on the Stock Exchange and who left his country to live in Papeete. Lucy's white employer praises the expatriate Frenchman's depiction of Tahiti which Mariah ethnocentrically assumes is virtually synonymous and interchangeable with Antigua. But Lucy's dry comment about gender and class difference implies the well-known tales of Gauguin's sexual activity that resulted in his death.

> Of course his life could be found in the pages of a book; I had just begun to notice that the lives of men always are. He was shown to be a man rebelling against an established order he had found corrupt; and even though he was doomed to defeat—he died an early death—he had the perfume of the hero about him. I was not a man; I was a young woman from the fringes of the world, and when I left my home I had wrapped around my shoulders the mantle of a servant. (95)

With the best intentions, Mariah introduces Lucy to a painter whose canvases are peopled (Mariah thinks) by women like Lucy. In Lucy's view, however, Paul Gauguin is a cultural interventionist in Tahiti who became famous for painting representations that reflect an ethnocentric gaze. Mariah's inability to understand Lucy's ire reaffirms the psychological damage and economic exploitation that Mariah's ignorance perpetuates. Having identified herself as someone living on the fringes of the household, Lucy goes on to admire the marginalization of artists she meets at a party. Yet when the party's host, another Paul, fetishizes her hair and treats her as an exotic object—he views Lucy from a vantage point that incorporates Gauguin's gaze—everyone at the party rapidly understands that she now occupies a role marked out by him: "It was understood that when everyone left, I would not leave with them" (100). To what extent she is a willing partner and goes along with being singled out by the host is left up in the air.—Lucy the implication goes—now repositions herself and watches the guests file out from the party. In a sense, she reverses their gaze and lets the drama play itself out.

Further, she brings together the sexual-intertextual dimension of Gauguin's behavior toward Tahitian women by inserting an old sexually-based tale from her past at this point, told to her by a childhood Antiguan acquaintance named Myrna. It concerns the death of a fisherman and Myrna's reaction to a series of incidents involving him:

> She told me that she had not been crying for Mr. Thomas at all—
> she had been crying for herself. She said that she used to meet
> Mr. Thomas . . . under a breadfruit tree that was near her latrine
> . . . at the back of her house, and she would stand in the dark,
> fully clothed but without her panties, and he would put his
> middle finger up inside her. . . . She and Mr. Thomas never spoke
> about it . . . After he had removed his finger from inside her . . .
> she said that she had not decided exactly what she was going to
> do with the money yet, but whatever it would be, she did not yet
> have enough. (104–105)

The vulnerable child succumbs to and even appears to secretly enjoy Mr. Thomas's physical abuse. He makes her feel special and she needs the money exchanged for her complicity. Lucy responds to this disturbing tale in an unexpected fashion: in her recollection, she is overcome with jealousy because the fisherman, Mr. Thomas, had singled out a "picky-haired girl" and not herself for "such an extraordinary thing." The last thing Lucy wants is to be ordinary.

The tale underscores Lucy's former frustrations and her mixed judgment; she longs to break out of roles, even if this escape must take place at the expense of her own body. Through the association of Mr. Thomas's hands with Paul's hands at the party as he rummages in a fish tank for a starfish-shaped rhinestone earring, Lucy connects sex, secrecy, oral narrative, and male-female relations. Paul represents a fake miniature version of Mr. Thomas, groping in a tank for a symbol of bourgeois living that emulates items of authentic tropical beauty. Perhaps with a touch of self-mockery he fishes for a glittering fake starfish.

Paul thus symbolically hints at Lucy's confused status by depicting her as an attractive but artificial starfish, an ornament that no longer belongs in the sea. The starfish is out of its element in a plastic world, no longer (in a sense) itself. Lucy's conflicted ontological status signals her growing resentment at being trapped. The moment of recognition that these images instigate heralds a moral cleansing on Lucy's part: "I began to feel like a dog on a leash, a long leash but a leash all the same" (110); "I was living in a home, though, and it was not my own" (112).

An intervention from Antigua, however, marks a drastic change in Lucy's life. Lucy's mother sends a letter about the death of her father, its arrival coinciding with Lucy's newly-found knowledge of Myrna's secret life. Although the letter is marked urgent, Lucy does not open it and responds to the inner strife it generates over motherhood and sexuality by buying a camera. As a culturally functional metaphor, the camera serves as a tool of self-appropriation for Lucy who is tired of expectations about the demands placed on her. As much as she can, Lucy makes it her business to reject any expropriation of her personhood that she does not herself choose. In that sense, the camera's gaze is empowering because it enables distances and defines a distinct place and space for the gazer.

The camera proffers the illusion that material reality can be controlled when Lucy blocks and reverses her mother's gaze across the Caribbean and the Pacific. She uses the camera through which she gazes unrestrictedly herself to redeploy her mother's watchfulness. Scopic discoveries substitute for the unpleasant visual images rendered by her memories of the past. With a camera, memories can be rearranged, boundaries elided; photos can be used to manipulate and conceal the real. Perhaps more to the point, photos can level the playing field between Lucy and those who would objectify her with their gazes: with a camera, the equalizer of distance is always present.

To augment her self-assertion, Lucy embarks on a chance sexual relationship with the Panamanian man who sells her the camera; yet he appears to her as a somewhat familiar person, perhaps a relative of her host family from the isle of Martinique. When Philip sells Lucy the camera, he qualifies as a co-conspirator of sorts, a mysterious other who somewhat resembles Lucy. Her quest for self-completion results in their brief affair which signifies both a "self-doubling" and a form of resistance to the maternal gaze.

Ultimately, Lucy reacts to her father's death with a railing letter to her mother: "I said that she had acted like a saint, but that since I was living in this real world I had really wanted just a mother" (127). Lucy opts to claim her sexuality as she pleases and to fly in the face of colonialism's desire to control "the natives," a desire that Lucy's mother mimics. In rejecting the maternal injunctions that one sees in such previous novels as *At the Bottom* and *Annie John*, the protagonist of *Lucy* consciously articulates a form of postcolonial resistance. She has come to hate her biological mother, she says, although this pronouncement is continually undercut by professions of love. What she has come to hate is the colonizing project that seeks to contain her. She will not be part of the imperial narrative, a fact that is signaled by her recognition of the trauma of separation from both the biological and colonial mothers that her acts will entail. Her father's death frees her from speaking the patriarchal language of oppression and accepting its terms. She substitutes for it an emergent postcolonial code of her own devising that both reinscribes and resists the "law of the father."

The renegotiation of the conflict between the patriarch and the postcolonial daughter reaches a climax after another potent intervention. The same Paul whose white hand dived (like Mr. Thomas's) for a fake starfish now proudly shows Lucy around the countryside and specifically points out an old plantation as a landmark to be admired. Paul identifies with the spirit of adventure in any man who crosses "the great seas, not only to find riches, he said, but to feel free, and this search for freedom was part of the whole human situation" (*Lucy* 129). He scarcely notices the dead animals littering the highway around them, killed by fast cars. Lucy vehemently reacts to Paul's blithe fantasy of colonial adventurism, refusing any longer to speak the patriarchal language of oppression: "I tried to put a light note in my voice as I said, 'On their way to freedom. some people find riches, some people find death,' but I did not succeed" (129).

After Lucy tells Mariah about her trip with Paul, Mariah connects Lucy's anger to her feelings about her mother. As Lucy is coming to (re-) create herself, so Mariah probes newly-found psychological depths, as if in a healthy mimicking gesture. Lucy confesses how angry she felt when she learned of her mother's plans for her male siblings' future education and professional careers. She confides that a "sword pierce[d] her heart": "To myself I [Lucy] then began to call her [Annie John's mother] Mrs. Judas, and I began to plan a separation from her that even then I suspected would never be complete" (130–131).

Lucy acts as if she wants to throw off two massive weights at once: the gendered, personal burden of knowing how her family favored her brothers which is inextricably fused with the burden of living as a female in a colonized country. She finds both forms of authority treacherous; both mothers have become, in her eyes, a pair of "Mrs. Judases." The collection of birth and postnatal memories that Lucy recounts to Mariah underscores the fusion of the two mothers. In the first instance, colonized Antigua meshes with her old home life in a scenario that flaunts the colors of the Union Jack, keen signs of colonial exploitation:

> the color of six o'clock in the evening sky on the day I went to call the midwife to assist my mother in the birth of my first brother; the white of the chemise that my mother embroidered for the birth of my second brother; the redness of the red ants that attacked my third brother as he lay in bed next to my mother a day after he was born; the navy blue of the sailor suit my first brother wore when my father took him to a cricket match; the absence of red lipstick on my mothers mouth after they were all born. (131)

These memories, inflected with violence and hues of domination, bring Lucy up short in her attempt to tell how desire for her mother conflicts with maternal demands: "But I couldn't speak, so I couldn't tell her that my mother was my mother and that society and history and culture and other women in general were something else altogether" (131–132). At this point, with the best ethnocentric will in the world, Mariah gives Lucy a copy of Simone de Beauvoir's philosophical treatise on sexual politics, *The Second Sex*, understood by Lucy as another representation of cultural imperialism that signs Mariah unmistakably as part of the colonizing project. Lucy knows full well how Mariah has "completely misinterpreted my situation" (132). Having unburdened her problems with motherhood and colonial intervention on to Mariah, Mariah then exchanges for this knowledge a famous bourgeois feminist text embedded in eurocentric beliefs and principles.

Lucy may fall silent here before the contradictions inherent in her plight as biological and cultural post-colonial subject, but elsewhere, she implicitly notes connections between her dual sense of personal and political estrangement. She observes the everyday objects around her and provides instances of political and cultural subjugation almost in the same breath as the imagery moves from daffodils and minions to plowed fields and cameras. This self-critical use of language, this hybrid form—the self-knowledge implied in growing up "fragmented"—yields a decolonizing of the mind. She claims the right to what Edward Said calls "the audacious metaphoric charting of spiritual territory usurped by colonial masters" ("Figures" 6).

For example, Lucy sentimentally relates a story about how she used to think life would have been preferable if the French and not the British had been colonizers. She reasons that the French stamps she received from a pen pal bore a seemingly more progressive message: "The stamps on her letter were always canceled with the French words for liberty, equality, and fraternity; on mine there was no such words, only the image of a stony-face, sour-mouth woman" (136). In her evolving maturity, however, Lucy shies away from that preference, but still with some reservations: "I understand that, in spite of those words, my pen pal and I were in the same boat; but still I think those words have a better ring to them than the image of a stony-face, sour-mouth woman (136). This seemingly "innocent" commentary on stamps strikes an explicitly political chord, revealing Lucy's love of justice as well as her ironic sense (suggesting that she has not completely internalized anti-colonialist opposition) that the "face" of colonialism is utterly separated from its discourse.

In the final section of the novel, Lucy asserts that she is "making a new beginning again" (133). In recollecting and summarizing her past, she pointedly rehearses her origins and the interventions of Christopher Columbus, thus forging an intertextual relation between her own foundations and the exploits of the imperial explorer. In her own ironic words, [he committed a] "foul deed, a task like that would have killed a thoughtful person, but he went on to live a very long life" (135). Subsequently, Lucy tells the story of refusing to stand up and sing "Rule Britannia" at school, attributing her disobedience to the unattractiveness of Britons and the fact that "I was not a Briton and that until not too long ago I would have been a slave" (135). In school at the time, her action was not deemed especially scandalous (because it was expected, presumably); "instead, my choir mistress only wondered if all their efforts to civilize me over the years would come to nothing in the end" (135).

She then rehearses her life up to the present: "I had begun to see the past like this: there is a line, you can draw . . . yourself, or sometimes it gets drawn for you" (137). She wants to be a woman shedding illusion instead of feeling "like a dog on a leash, a long leash but a leash all the same" (110). She sees through Paul ("I could have told him that I had sized him up" [156]) and her friend Peggy in terms of colonial mimicry:

> Her hair smelled of lemons—not real lemons, not lemons as I
> knew them to smell, not the sort of lemons that grew in my yard
> at home, but artificial lemons, made up in a laboratory. Peggy did
> not know what a real lemon smelled like. How am I going to get
> out of this? (154–155)

But the resolutions to these problematic insights are not yet fully available to Lucy: "I quickly placed a big rock on top of it" [her feelings of being trapped] (155). She does, however, pride herself on seeing the sheer ordinariness beneath Lewis's veneer of superiority: his character is summed up in his perverse final present to the environmentally conscious Mariah of a coat made of animal fur. She sees that the family members scarcely know her, although they consider it their (First World) right to "know" and, therefore, control her. With no way of undoing the infinite play of dissimulation and self-deception, they scarcely see beyond the accidents of Lucy's differently curled hair and a deeper shade of complexion.

Nonetheless, Lucy will not forgive her mother for an accumulation of perceived wrongs, especially the psychological neglect of Lucy herself, so she sends her a phony forwarding address. In contrast, she is willing to rationalize Mariah's fury when Lucy says she will leave: "Her voice was full of anger, but I ignored it. It's always hard for the person who is left behind" (141). She is even willing to forgive Mariah the mark of the colonizer; apparently, the trauma of separation has not forced total alienation upon Lucy:

> Mariah spoke to me harshly all the time now, and she began to
> make up rules which she insisted that I follow . . . It was a last

> resort for her—insisting that I be the servant and she the
> master. . . . The master business did not become her at all, and
> it made me sad to see her that way. (143)

Interpreting Mariah's behavior positively, Lucy practices restraint—the kind
she cannot extend toward her mother. She evinces compassion. The implied
link between Lucy's compassion for a colonial mother in Mariah and the
absence of compassion toward her biological mother evades Lucy's grasp at
this point. But she verges on an understanding of that link when she reap-
plies knowledge gleaned from her mother at home; the complexity of Lucy's
feelings are also evident in her desire to use that knowledge in explaining to
Mariah that her "'situation is an everyday thing. Men behave in this way all
the time. . . .' But I knew . . . she would have said, 'What a cliche.' But all the
same, where I came from, every woman knew this cliche, and a man like
Lewis would not have been a surprise" (141). Lucy recognizes that her
knowledge of Antiguan mores has empowered her to avoid Mariah's
dangerous innocence. In a nifty parthian shot, moreover, she terms Mariah a
stony-faced woman, echoing earlier descriptions of Queen Elizabeth II as, "a
stony-faced, sour-mouth woman" (136). She slowly begins to discern finer
distinctions among Mariah, Lewis, and her own mother, or rather, using a
self-preserving tactic, she begins to judge them in terms of their attitudes
toward colonialism. Lucy has turned the tables against the family that sought
to control her. As far as she is economically able to do so, she begins to
control her own environment, right down to sexual encounters. She fractures
any attachment between sexuality and the damaging force of empire.

Toward the end, Lucy names who she is. She recites her given name
and the names she attempts to adopt: Lucy, Lucifer, Josephine Potter—
names associated with plantocratic lineage, slave traders, (the English Potter
family), and a Western symbol of evil. She imagines the possibilities of other
names—Emily, Charlotte, Jane, and Enid. These names clearly evoke white
female heroines such as Jane Eyre who lives in a house with an imprisoned
white Caribbean woman, (as well as the creator of them both, Charlotte
Bronte, and her sister Emily), and Enid Blyton, notorious in Britain for her
racist characterizations in children's books.

In the name "Lucifer" and the allusion to the "lost paradise" of Lucy's
innocence, Lucy embraces the oppositional name wholeheartedly. Lucifer is
configured, after all, as the perfect Western villain. Lucy finds part of her
postcolonial identity in this name:

> It was the moment I knew who I was. . . . Lucy, a name for
> Lucifer. That my mother would have found me devil-like did not

surprise me, for I often thought of her as god-like, and are not the child of gods devils? I did not grow to like the name Lucy— I would have much preferred to be called Lucifer outright—but whenever I saw my name I always reached out to give it a strong embrace. (152–153)

In these namings, Lucy has begun to dispense with surrogates, positively announcing to herself a personal capacity to abandon not just Mariah and Peggy, but Jane and Enid too. Her names empower her to break her dependency on others, her compliances, her catering to them, and even her continuing resistance to old emotional ties (Belenky et al. 83–86).

The notebook that Mariah gives Lucy as a farewell present enables her to reverse the colonial project since the notebook visually signs patriotism in its red, white, and blue composition. These nationalist associations refer back to the fall of Rome mentioned earlier, but this time Lucy is the vandal who conquers the original invaders. She will use the mark of the colonizer on behalf of the postcolonial agitators. The blank pages of her life that now stretch before her, like the potential but unused frames of a camera spool, stand a better chance of being imprinted authentically. The conscious articulation of a desire—"I wish I could love someone so much that would I die from it" (164)—complicates her past, present and future. Yet her resistance to the grand narratives of marriage, religion, and cultural conformity persists. She begins to confront herself.

By the end of the novel, having come to recognize the tunnel vision of the homogeneous imperative, Lucy is on the way to self-articulation. Now she sees that it is not only the colonizer who imposes the disfiguring mark of the dominant culture. These recognitions recall Lucy's trickster story of the monkey who retaliated when Lucy's mother, irritated by the monkey's stares, threw stones at it. Just as Lewis's monkey metonymizes Lucy, so the monkey who permanently scars Lucy's mother is an insurgent who refuses to be controlled (154–155). At the level of mini-anecdote, Kincaid's texts are paradigmatic of a quest for independence and freedom both personal and political. But the pursuit of this quest results in the attainment of a precarious state of being, and Lucy recognizes her own uneasiness regarding it: "I am alone in the world. It was not a small accomplishment. I thought I would die doing it. I was not happy, but that seemed too much to ask for" (161). Still, having arrived at this complex moment, she can now love Mariah on her own terms, no longer so confused about Mariah as a substitute mother or her own ability to love without encumbrance. The earlier persuasive words of her biological mother have "ceased to mean" (Bakhtin 425). She is becoming comfortable with all the parts of herself:

I had seen Mariah. She had asked me to come and have dinner
with her. We were friends again; we said how much we missed
each other's company. She looked even more thin that usual. She
was alone, and she felt lonely. . . . When we said goodbye, I did
not know if I would ever see her again. (162–163)

The camera which has served as the medium of the gaze ultimately
serves to trace Lucy's maturation. In a graphic domestic scene she sees:

a picture of my dresser top with my dirty panties and lipstick, an
unused sanitary napkin, and an open pocketbook scattered
about; a picture of a necklace made of strange seeds, which I had
bought from a woman on the street; a picture of a vase I had
bought at the museum, a reproduction of one found at the site
of a lost civilization. (121)

In preparation for the act of writing—the act of self-inscription— she states:
"I did all sorts of little things; I washed my underwear, scrubbed the stove,
washed the bathroom floor, trimmed my nails, arranged my dresser, made
sure I had enough sanitary napkins" (163). Crucially, the second mention of
the sanitary napkins, emblems of maturation, are no longer confined by the
camera's eye, no longer one of the signs of a chaotic or fragmented existence.
Lucy will prepare her affairs as she pleases; she is no longer the object of the
gaze, but the orchestrator of her own life. Her menstrual blood links her not
only to life and maturation, but to Mariah's present, the blood-red Italian
notebook, a mark of creativity, self-inscription, and survival.
      Jamaica Kincaid's fiction invariably achieves closure in terms of water
that cleanses, fertilizes dry ground, and opens up new radical possibilities.
Symbolically, water is also a place of indeterminacy where anything can
happen: it signifies Lucy's return to amniotic fluid and new beginnings. As
the beautiful Caribbean represents her as a black Antiguan and a colonial
subject, so now does the ink in her pen; she is the community recorder who
connects her life in Antigua with what lies ahead; linking the personal and
political dimensions of her life, she displays the effect of colonialism and
postcolonialism on an African-Caribbean woman. As the final sentence of
the novel suggests, her weeping is a form of erasure: "as I looked at this
sentence [about loving someone so much she would die] a great wave of
shame came over me and I wept so much that the tears fell on the page and
caused all the words to become one great big blur" (164).
      On the one hand, talking about water, arriving at it, finding comfort in
it returns Lucy to a time of harmony and safety. On the other, Lucy is forced

to abide with a watery indeterminacy, "one great big blur" that militates against hard and fast answers. The image of the blur suggests that everything is out of focus; it returns us to a camera metaphor, but one connoting a confusion coupled with determinacy. In Lucy's more mature vision, the oscillation of meanings signifies that nothing is privileged, resolved, or closed off. Through the metaphor of water, Lucy contextualized the metaphor she used previously when she observed Mariah acting in her normal manner, "which was that the world was round and we all agreed on that"; now Lucy knows symbolically that the world is flat and she can fall off if she ventures to the edge. She knows the fraudulence of the overall "consensus" that Mariah is so sure of, and its relation to a blonde, European world, the one that Peggy tries to simulate with her artificial lemon shampoo. In questioning "roundness" and stepping closer to the edge, Lucy realizes she can see both forwards and backwards. Having refused enclosures built by others, she begins to forge a site (sight) of her own. She refuses assimilation and embraces cultural difference and an "alien status," only partly of her own making, in the margins (hooks 23).

In this enactment of cultural revenge, of the dissolution of authority, Lucy claims her right to feel and to drown out cognition for the time being. Revealing the duplicity of the colonizing economy by mapping herself on to earlier texts, she creates a new postcolonial cartography. She is ready to write. Finally, at a symbolic level, Lucy is also Antigua of 1967, a territory freeing itself from the colonizer. In the late nineteen sixties, Antigua was struggling toward partial independence and the United States was becoming a contestational zone of anti-war protesters, just as Lucy struggles successfully toward a form of independence. By the end of the narrative, Lucy has begun to decolonize herself; in that sense, Jamaica Kincaid, a postcolonial subject in her own right, has made an ex-post facto intervention in the description of a colonized subject about to be legally and personally freed. The death-like, gray-black and cold January of the opening transitional period has been transformed through Lucy's awakening and agency into the blood-red, milk-white, Caribbean-blue colors of her writing.

PATRICIA ISMOND

Jamaica Kincaid: "First They Must Be Children"

The earliest phase of Caribbean writing, fighting to claim an identity for the black man, began with a sense of his damaged psyche. Among some of the writers who have emerged since then, there is a noticeable shift to another area of exploration They seem intent on affirming the character and spirit that were being forged in the region even while its peoples underwent the ills and privations of the past. They search out this character in the substance of family relationships, the urgencies of caring, sacrifice and struggle experienced at close domestic levels, and fostering courage and human values.

The trend is noticeable in writers from the French and English-speaking Caribbean (militancy seems to be the dominant trend in the Spanish contingent, though that topic is outside the scope of this paper). In Joseph Zobel's *Black Shack Alley* (1974) the young boy grows up in the love and sacrifice of his grandmother, and it is what equips him for life. Simone Schwarz-Bart in *The Bridge of Beyond* (1972) presents a similar theme: Telumée Miracle finds a bridge to her own self-achievement as an independent woman in her grandmother's fortitude and wisdom. The contribution of the Antiguan writer, Jamaica Kincaid, with whom this paper is concerned, also fits into this trend. Kincaid, writing from the metropolitan world of New York, returns exclusively to the childhood experience of growing up in

From *World Literature Written in English*, Autumn 1988. © 1988 by Patricia Ismond.

Antigua. She has lived most of her adult life away from that setting; but it is to this childhood experience that she returns to find the possibilities of a creative adjustment to a world and time so different in its ethos.

Jamaica Kincaid made an immediate impact on the literary scene when she first appeared in the early 1980s. Her two works so far are *At the Bottom of the River*, published in 1983, followed by *Annie John* in 1985. Annie John is a semi-autobiographical novel dealing with her experience of growing up in Antigua. *At the Bottom of the River* is a collection of pieces combining reflection and memories of that early experience. The two works are in fact companion pieces, the one in straightforward prose, the other poetic and intuitional in style. The substance of the experience in *Annie John* reappears in the images of *At the Bottom of the River*.

The reader is immediately struck by the originality of Kincaid's work, an originality that comes both from the peculiar character of the experience she recalls as from her singular rendering of it. In the more accessible *Annie John*, she re-creates a vivid picture of the Antiguan setting in which she grew up. It is the typical small-island environment before urban times. The conditions and lifestyle around the capital town of St. John's are still provincial. There are wooden shingle houses, their yards equipped with the inevitable breadfruit trees and the heap of stones for bleaching clothes; kerosene lamps have not yet been replaced by electricity. The men earn a living as fishermen and small craftsmen (Annie John's father is a carpenter); the women are devoted to caring for their men and children and keeping house. The people still hold to their belief in obeah cures, superstitions and bush baths. At the same time, parents who are not too badly off strive to bring up their girls "to be a lady" according to the norms of Sunday school culture. Kincaid recalls the "manners lady" to whom one was sent for lessons in etiquette (*Annie John* 28).

This particular variety of small-island living is different in temper from that of a George Lamming, for example. It is not quite the restive plantation milieu of a Creighton village (*In the Castle of My Skin*); it is self-contained and effectively shut off from the realities of race and class. The atmosphere is one not of privation, but of spare essentials. For the child growing up in that setting, life revolved mainly around school and home. The familial and domestic tend to dominate life in this kind of environment; in Kincaid's case, home and setting were indistinguishable from each other, as this comment suggests: "I identified parental restrictiveness with the restrictiveness of my surroundings" (Kincaid/De Vries 41). This experience of home, as Annie John records, centred especially on the figure of her mother. Kincaid's memory clings to that focal experience of her mother, and her work deals extensively with growing up in that close childhood relationship between herself and her mother.

The attachment must have been all the more intense for one who remained an only child up to the age of nine. The prominent role of her mother in her life, however, also harks back to a common feature of West Indian family life documented by Edith Clarke in *My Mother Who Fathered Me* (1957). Clarke showed how the prevailing types of conjugal relationships in West Indian society conspired to place the onus of responsibility for children on the mother, and left the father relatively free of parental obligation. Annie John recalls being hastily gathered into her mother's skirts whenever they passed "one of the women that my father had loved and with whom he had had a child or children" (17). The father of these removed connections did not "belong" as fully as she and her mother belonged together. Add to this the fact that boys were banished from the world of a lady-like upbringing and we get the background to a curious feature in Kincaid: the figure of the woman remains deeply impressed on her consciousness. The image of the other, what she idealizes as well as resists, always appears in the form of a woman.

The particular circumstances of her background, therefore, and no doubt qualities of her own temperament, helped to deepen the seminal bond between mother and child. Revisiting that childhood, Kincaid gives testimony of the powerful ties between mother and child in what must rank among the most penetrating studies on the subject so far. *Annie John* traces the various stages of her progress from childhood to adolescence in terms of this relationship with her mother. It began with the fullness of maternal love, care and nurturing in infancy. The experience of being "weaned," a sundering between herself and her mother, marked the passage to girlhood. So that growing up and beginning to fend for herself meant an experience of increasing disfavour with her mother, presaging a silent opposition and undeclared war between them.

Her mother, in effect, was the medium through which she entered her first world. She provided her with her earliest glimpses of the bigger world; she was the one most responsible for initiating her into the inner areas of self by arousing those complex emotions and sensitivities associated with the experience of growing up. The deeply embedded sense of her mother was to follow her down the years, retaining the painful doubleness of the early period. Kincaid-Annie John recalls her early prescience of this in the novel: "For I could not be sure when it was really my mother, and when it was really her shadow standing between me and the rest of the world" (107).

"My Mother," an outstanding sequence in *At the Bottom of the River*, is the mythologized burden of *Annie John*. It plots her progress through life in terms of this sense of her mother, to take the form of a journey extending from childhood right into the present struggle for survival. The first piece tells of the painful necessity of being weaned from total dependence on her

mother, and the submerged tensions and hostilities that entered their relationship from that time.

> Placing her arms around me, she drew my head closer and closer
> to her bosom, until finally I suffocated. I lay on her bosom,
> breathless, for a time uncountable, until one day, for a reason she
> has kept to herself, she shook me out and stood me under a tree
> and I started to breathe again. I cast a sharp glance at her and said
> to myself, "So." Instantly I grew my own bosoms, small mounds
> at first, leaving a small soft place between them, where if ever
> necessary, I could rest my own head. Between my mother and me
> now were the tears I had cried, and I gathered up some stones
> and banked them in so that they formed a small pond. The water
> in the pond was thick and black and poisonous, so that only
> unnameable invertebrates could live in it. My mother and I now
> watched each other carefully, always making sure to shower the
> other with words and deeds of love and affection. (53–54)

The strange movement of imagery here is remarkably direct and literal
in its impact: it is almost as if the feelings and incidents she recalls actually
registered in that way. This particular piece has been quoted at length
because it gives a clear insight into the underlying sources and dynamic of
Kincaid's style, especially in *At the Bottom of the River.* We are taken with
childlike simplicity and spontaneous fantasy into what emerges as the dream-
scape of the subconscious. Images and fragments from favourite children's
stories, and strong personal symbols from Kincaid's childhood surface in the
memory of that experience. Thus, the "pond of tears" separating her from
her mother is reminiscent of Alice's "pool of tears" in *Alice in Wonderland;*
while the image of being "shook out and stood under a tree" survives from
the memory of being sent out to eat her dinner under the breadfruit trees
whenever she was being punished (*Annie John* 12, 18). These images hark
back to the child's original acceptance of the world of fantasy and symbol.
One factor is of special significance here. The climate of local superstition
and obeah practices in which Kincaid grew up had a lasting influence in
deepening these impulses towards the fantastical. These extend, increasingly
as the sequence unfolds, into the surreal accesses of dream.

Following on this initial crisis of estrangement, the relationship with
her mother becomes one in which she must struggle for her very survival.
Subsequent stages of the journey see her engaged in a trickster-like effort to
outstrip and leave her mother's influence safely behind her ("I had hoped to
see my mother permanently cemented to the seabed"). She later succumbs to

the inescapable destiny of their journey "down the valley" together—an unhappy compromise whose bitter traces leave "in [their] trail, small colonies of worms." It is a process of increasing strife and trial, until she finds her way to an envisioned reconciliation with her mother, evoked in this paradisal movement:

> My mother and I live in a bower made from flowers whose petals are imperishable. There is the silvery blue of the sea, crisscrossed with sharp darts of light, there is the warm rain falling on the clumps of castor bush, there is the small lamb bounding across the pasture . . . It is in this way my mother and I have lived for a long time now. (61)

The child-mother relationship thus deepens into an ultimate significance in Kincaid's imagination. It is a paradigm of the struggle between the self and the other, the tug between the yearning for completion and all outside us that seem to resist it, provoking, as Kincaid tells us, the will to master or be mastered. Beneath this struggle lies the final need for union. Kincaid's journey thus recovers an authentic mythic level in "My Mother": the loss of innocence and security, initiation into experience, and the struggle to regain that innocence.

Kincaid remains close to the child's modes of perception and language in these renderings. The roots of her style, as earlier noted, lie in the child's instinct for fantasy; the free play between its imaginings and the world of fact; its spontaneous connections between widely different spheres and categories; and the natural simplicity with which it does all this. We are almost in the presence of the writer-child, as one reviewer puts it (Ozick). Kincaid seems to have retained the child-faculty intact. Repossessing it in her adult years, she authenticates and affirms the power of the imagination of childhood. What has crystallized in this child-language extends into a number of powerful visionary modes in Kincaid's hands. There are accesses of clairvoyance and divination, of the prophetic and apocalyptic in her work. In a piece entitled "At Last" from *The Bottom of the River* she reflects on the irreducible essence of things, despite the world according to science and technology. The passage in question attains prophetic, biblical force, while we still hear the voice of the child: "Will the hen, stripped of its flesh, its feathers scattered perhaps to the four corners of the earth, its bones molten and sterilized, one day speak? And what will it say? I was a hen? I had twelve chicks? One of my chicks, named Beryl, took a fall?" (18)

The preoccupation with childhood lies at the core of Kincaid's work and represents a very special achievement. In exploring it, she renews our understanding of the meaning of innocence and the value and possibilities of our first world. The line which I have chosen as my title appears as a prophetic refrain in one of the movements of *At the Bottom of the River* ("Wingless"): "First they must be children." It gathers echoes of the New Testament. One must look closely at what she recognizes in this innocence. It is not a state free from stain and imperfection. Growing up in *Annie John* involves an openness and receptivity to all manner of emotions and impulses, creative and destructive—love, dawning cruelty, generosity, possessiveness, instincts of hubris. In other words, the child is fully in touch with the complex motions of her own nature and being. It is also the freedom of the child's natural curiosity, the intentness with which it relates to the world around it, animate and inanimate forms alike. In Kincaid's testimony, the mother comes to contain and embody the world because of the totality with which the child lived that first relationship with her; and the struggle to be reconciled with her mother contained in embryo the struggle to be reconciled with life itself. In another piece entitled "Blackness," Kincaid intimates the possibilities and depths of remaining in touch with these sources as she, now a mother, looks through the prism of her own child. The image is, as it were, twice reflected:

> [My child] traces each thing from its meagre happenstance beginnings in cool and slimy marsh, to its great glory and dominance of air or land or sea, to its odd remains entombed in mysterious alluviums . . . She feels the specter, first cold, then briefly warm, then cold again as it passes from atmosphere to atmosphere. Having observed the many differing physical existences feed on each other, she is beyond despair or the spiritual vacuum. (51)

And what has all this to do with Kincaid's roots in the Caribbean? Derek Walcott, in an early response to Kincaid's work, has this to say: "Genius has many surprises, and one of them is geography." Kincaid grew up in an environment which helped give her a firm grounding in human relationships and their tenacity, an uncluttered landscape which kept her imagination in touch with primal realities. Her own work is proof of the power of that landscape. In reclaiming these roots she makes an explicit disavowal of the universe according to the twentieth-century view—a system that can be calculated, programmed and mastered, where the human spirit is left very little space to breathe. She puts it thus as she looks through the vision reflected at the bottom of the river: "the sun was The Sun, a creation of Benevolence and Purpose and not a star among many stars, with a predictable cycle and a predictable end . . ." (*At the Bottom of the River* 77). In the global scheme of things, Kincaid's native Caribbean, despite the brutalities of its past, is yet close to the state of childhood, and has the capacity to bring this message.

SUSAN SNIADER LANSER

Compared to What? Global Feminism, Comparatism, and the Master's Tools

And rain is the very thing that you, just now, do not want, for you are thinking of the hard and cold and dark and long days you spent working in North American (or worse, Europe), earning some money so that you could stay in this place (Antigua) where the sun always shines and where the climate is deliciously hot and dry . . . and since you are on your holiday, since you are a tourist, the thought of what it might be like for someone who had to live day in, day out in a place that suffers constantly from drought . . . must never cross your mind.

And you leave, and from afar you watch as we do to ourselves the very things you used to do to us. And you might feel that there was more to you than that, you might feel that you had understood the meaning of the Age of Enlightenment (though, as far as I can see, it has done you very little good); you loved knowledge, and wherever you went you made sure to build a school, a library (yes, and in both of these places you distorted or erased my history and glorified your own).

As for what we were like before we met you, I no longer care. No periods of time over which my ancestors held sway, no documentation of complex civilisations, is any comfort to me. Even if I really came from people who were living like monkeys in trees, it was better to be that than what happened to me, what I became after I met you.

—Jamaica Kincaid, *A Small Place*

A few years ago at the lake where I spend my summers, I read Jamaica Kincaid's brilliantly disturbing book *A Small Place*, a pain-filled and searing

From *Borderworks*. © 1994 by Cornell University Press.

indictment of racist colonialism and its perpetuation both in postcolonial corruption and in the tourism that brings 10 million people to the Caribbean each year. Since this book began unsettling me, it has attached itself to questions, texts, and topoi that are in various ways comparative, an appropriate consequence since *A Small Place* is "comparative literature" in the most literal sense: a literary work that makes (cultural) comparisons. Although the cover blurbs engage *A Small Place* in predominantly male canonical intertext (as "Swiftian," as a "jeremiad," as resembling the "Ancient Mariner"), I compare it to writings in which women criticize national and imperial policies. Virginia Woolf's *Three Guineas* (1938), the novels of Christa Wolf (1968-89), Audre Lorde's essay on the invasion of Grenada (1984), *The History of Mary Prince, A West Indian Slave* (1831), and Toni Morrison's *Beloved* (1987). I have wondered about the differences in tone and stance between *A Small Place* and Kincaid's fiction, about the ways in which readers—black and white, male and female, U.S. and Antiguan—have responded to this book, about the different implications conveyed by its publisher's classification (black studies), and by the Library of Congress catalogue (Antigua—Description and travel). *A Small Place* has helped to redirect my thinking about eighteenth-century women writers, to attend to the traces of colonialism in "domestic" fictions such as Isabelle de Charrière's *Lettres de Mistriss Henley* (1784) and Sarah Scott's *Millenium Hall* (1762), to explore the ways in which François de Grafigny's Peruvian princess (1747) reverses the tropes of empire when she names the Europeans "savages" and "barbarians" and the tropes of fiction when she refuses to marry the heroic Frenchman who has befriended her. My research on eighteenth-century women critics has turned toward the relationship between social values and theories of literature as I ask, for example, whether the dismaying conjunction of feminism and racism in Clara Reeve's *Plans of Education* (1792) has any relevance to her conception of the novel in *The Progress of Romance* (1785).

A Small Place has also led me to questions of personal and professional urgency that are less directly textual. I have reexamined real and imagined travel plans. I have asked myself whether there might be resemblances between tourists and comparatists: both "cosmopolitans" who pride ourselves on transcending narrow and parochial interests, who dwell mentally in one or two (usually Western) countries, summer metaphorically in a third, and visit other places for brief interludes. And I continue to struggle with the implications of *A Small Place* for my own position as a professional woman privileged to write this essay on a screened porch in the Maine woods ten feet from a lake that overlooks the White Mountains, one of the welcomed but sometimes resented "summer people" in an economically pressed rural community, asking myself what I must not dwell on to be here and what I can return to this small place for the peace and renewal it gives more generously to me than to its own hardworking citizens, few of whom have long summer vacations and houses ten feet from the lake.

These questions that *A Small Place* has raised for me are comparative questions, but they are not by and large the questions with which comparative literature has taught me to concern myself, nor is *A Small Place* the kind of text I have been trained to "compare." I have been a feminist for as long as I have been a comparatist, but my work as a feminist has not had much *formal* assistance from comparative literature as such. For although there has been feminist comparative practice for as long as there have been feminist critics, and although influential feminist theorists from Kate Millett to Gayatri Spivak were trained as comparatists, comparative literature as a self-conscious and self-articulating discipline has remained relatively untouched by feminist scholarship. Even so current a collection as Clayton Koelb and Susan Noakes's *Comparative Perspective on Literature* (1988), which includes three manifestly feminist essays among its twenty-one pieces, does not integrate feminism into its theorizing of the discipline. For what I hope to demonstrate are related reasons, although "East-West" studies have become more common and "third world" literatures are "emerging" into Western syllabi, comparative literature as practiced in the West (and sometimes in the "East") remains, as Koelb and Noakes rightly remark of their own collection, "skewed heavily toward Europe and indeed toward the canonical writers of a few particularly well studied European languages." In comparing white men to white men from white men's vantage points, comparative literature as it is normatively practiced has attached itself in powerfully stubborn ways to what Audre Lorde has called "the master's tools."

Although it is comparative literature and not feminist studies on which this essay concentrates, I acknowledge that feminist criticism has tended to be as insufficiently comparatist as comparative literature has been insufficiently feminist. Whereas Western comparatism has sometimes engaged in feminist practice without significantly disturbing the theoretical foundations of the discipline, academic Western feminism has, conversely, theorized itself as comparative (that is, as concerned with women across or beyond national and cultural boundaries) without engaging significantly in comparative practices. Feminist criticism has tended to claim as universal what is particular (for example, using "nineteenth-century women" to describe white educated women of England and the United States) or has (increasingly) "included" other literatures without knowing the languages and cultures in which these works originate. This means that neither feminist nor comparatist studies, as generally practiced in U.S. universities, is sufficiently comparative despite each field's commitment virtually by definition to difference as a primary concern. When I criticize both of these fields, I include my own scholarship, which reflects the Eurocentrism of my training and against which I am now struggling, like many others of my generation, to reeducate myself. I have been especially conscious of these limitations in completing my "comparative" study of women writers and narrative voice, which remains restrictively Western even though it "includes" African American literature.

It is not my purpose here to discuss why feminism has been inadequately comparative aside from noting that many U.S. feminist critics are not trained in either "foreign" languages or comparative inquiry (which I distinguish from the inclusion of difference). Rather, it is my intention in this essay to look at comparatism through the lens of (global) feminism in order to ask why comparative literature, which has so often been proudly open and avant-garde, has lagged behind related disciplines in its institutional response to feminist scholarship. I then suggest some premises for transforming the discipline that rely for theoretical support on "borderworks" such as *A Small Place* which are concerned with questions of globalism and nationalism, gender and race, literature and culture, difference and dominance. I hope through this project to make clear why I think comparatism and feminism are necessary not only for each other's institutional and intellectual health but for each one's integrity as a discipline and indeed for the still urgent mission Virginia Woolf framed in the 1930s: how we can "enter the professions and yet remain civilized human beings," human beings who "will teach the young to hate war."

That this volume is the first to raise feminist questions about comparative literature long after other fields have been challenged and reformed already suggests the "small place" feminism has occupied in theorizing the discipline. The lack of pressure feminism has exerted on comparative literature may in part reflect the discipline's laissez-faire tendencies. The postwar expansion of comparative literature to embrace virtually any study of literature beyond national boundaries has allowed a latitude of practice that may have forestalled a reconceptualization of the discipline. And because the field is vast and its scholars are often dispersed among many departments, comparatists tend to be genial about one another's work without necessarily seeing that work as having implications for their own. But such nonchalance could not fully explain why a computer search of the MLA bibliography for the entire 1980s, a decade when feminist criticism permeated literary scholarship, turned up among scores of entries in the category "Comparative Literature—Professional Topics," only one brief essay focused explicitly on feminism and comparative literature. Certainly it would not explain the virulent response that the feminist comparatist Evelyn Torton Beck received at a 1974 American Comparative Literature Association (ACLA) session when she spoke about gender issues in translation practices. It seems, rather, that comparative literature as it has traditionally been conceived may be incompatible with a global feminist project, that certain thoughts must not cross our consciousness, as they must not cross the Antiguan tourist's consciousness.

I want to press against this disciplinary repression with a large, provocative statement after the fashion of Kincaid; with an intensity that might be related to our institutional vulnerability, comparative literature has been resistant to global feminism because of its intersecting commitments to aestheticism and canonicity, tradition as longevity, theory as Continental philosophy, literature as intertext, and language as the Ur-ground of comparison—all of which reinforce a disciplinary ideology of transcendence and unity. As a result, comparatism has most often been a discourse of sameness even when it purports to be a discourse of difference.

The commitments of which I am speaking are abundantly documented in the comparative theory that build the discipline in Western Europe and the United States. Despite a certain interest in "folk" traditions in the nineteenth and early twentieth centuries, comparative literature has been preoccupied primarily with identifying, studying, and promoting the world's "great" literature. Its sense of authority is reflected, for example, in its traditional undergraduate mission to transmit "the major literary works of the western heritage," sometimes "enriched" by a few classical "Eastern" texts. These great works are to be viewed, as Renè Welleck put it, as "monuments" and not "documents," a position whose troubling underside is implied by Kincaid's observation that colonists build monuments to themselves among the colonized. These literary icons are protected from such disturbing deconstructions because they are read less in a context than in an intertext, since literature is understood to be produced by international literary movements according to universal literary "laws." The predominance of "influence" studies in comparative literature reflects this intertextual commitment most literally by presuming that works are what they are because of the (world) literature that has preceded them. "Minor" works are usually studied in relation to "major" ones—as *A Small Place* is validated by comparison to the "Ancient Mariner"—or in support of a universal textuality. Linguistic and political differences become "artificial . . . barriers" that have "confined the study of literature."

Such an environment easily defines out of greatness writings by women of all races—and men of some—that fail to satisfy white male norms or that lack visible comparative connections with traditional texts. Comparative literature's canons have "included" women primarily by selecting individual works (*The Tale of Genji, La Princesse de Clèves, Emma*) that conform to its aesthetic values and that can be studied without one's having to confront the kinds of questions feminists would ask. Although there has of course been some opening of the comparative canon, signs of anxiety and retrenchment remain. The 1989 ACLA report on undergraduate comparative literature professes (in negative syntax) to "welcome non-Western, women's literature and non-canonical literature" but insists that comparative literature must still ensure "some significant areas of expertise," thereby nullifying both the significance of these fields and the possibility that they are sites of expertise. In pleading that we "not forget also to introduce students to the canonical works upon which are based the prevailing sense of western culture," ACLA's curricular project would ensure that this "prevailing sense" not be challenged by a critique of Western culture such as *A Small Place*—which would surely also be dismissed as a document, not a monument.

Nor would *A Small Place* be considered "theory" in comparative literature's usual terms. In discussing the engagement with theory that marks the discipline, Koelb and Noakes include only men among the theorists whom comparatists might study alongside the "canonical writers of Western literature": "Marx, Freud, Lacan, Luhmann, Nietzsche, Wölfflin, Adorno, Derrida, Heidegger, Abraham and Torok, Louis Sullivan, and so on." Although surely Kristeva or Irigaray could have been mentioned, this list is disturbingly accurate: comparative literature does still understand "theory" in a Eurocentric and masculinist sense. "Great" theory is defined much like "great" literature: as cosmopolitan, Continental, verbally dense, concerned with what are taken to be 'large" and "universal" questions rather than "narrow" or "provincial" ones.

Consonant with its commitment to "great" literature and theory is comparative literature's commitment to long-lived text, a position in interesting tension with its sense of itself as intellectually avant-garde. The privileging of the traditional has created, for example, what Mary Louise Pratt calls a "selective multinationalism," by which comparative literature attends to classical Indian works such as the *Mahabharata* but not to the (more politically charged) writings of the colonial and postcolonial periods. This commitment to "traditional" literatures does not, however, override the Eurocentrism of comparatist studies, or courses in the history of criticism would routinely include Bharata's *Natyasastra*, the classic text of Sanskrit aesthetics, alongside Aristotle's *Poetics*. For comparatists the ultimate source of "Western tradition" remains ancient Greece, which at around the same time Goethe first called for a *Weltliteratur* was being reinvented as an Aryan culture against the evidence that its science, art, and philosophy result from "cultural mixtures" created by the Egyptians and Phoenicians who colonized Greece.

Obviously the predilection for "old" works and long-literate cultures implicitly devalues women's writings and "emergent" literatures. Robert Clements, for example, wrote in the late 1970s that although "Black African literature is of course the most visibly lacking component" in comparative literature, this absence is justified "since Africa has contributed fewer literary works that satisfy" the "dual criteria" of "international acclaim and enduring values" so tautologically constructed by comparative literature. On similar grounds, "massive areas, like Indonesia with a population of 100 million, would be minimally represented," though as a comparatist good sport Clements allowed "*aficionados* of African or Polynesian literatures . . . of course (to) feature them in theses written for their degrees." Obviously the world's geographic and literary "small places" haven't a chance against such practices by which only what is already deemed important to white men is worthy to be compared.

One reason Clements and other comparatists have given for excluding African or Polynesian literature is a linguistic one: Africans write in many languages, most of which are not known or taught in Western universities. This argument is easy enough to dismantle both by refusing comparative literature's Eurocentric linguistic hierarchies and by recalling the large body of African literature written in European languages. But it evokes a further reason why comparative literature remains resistant to both the global and the feminist: its insistence on language as a primary site of difference and hence not only the discipline's central basis for "comparison" but the very ground of its disciplinary legitimacy. It is not just that the overwhelmingly dominant languages of comparative literature study—indeed sometimes the only ones that fulfill graduate language requirements—are those of Western Europe or even a restrictive group of these, so that the field's language base is actually rather narrow and most comparatists can enjoy the comfort of having at least one "foreign" language in common. Equally problematic is the fact that the privileging of standard-language difference as the criterion for comparative study risks confusing linguistic knowledge with cultural knowledge and overlooks both cultural differences that are not visibly linguistic and linguistic differences that are not phonological. Reinhold Grimm has argued, for example, that in the Nazi period one could point to at least four "German literatures" without including the literatures of non-German countries such as Austria, and surely we would all agree with Walter Cohen that "in no two countries is English the same language." If we go further, we confront ramifications still more charged: the linguistic imperialism by which Janet Frame's New Zealand English is (mis)translated into American by her publishers; the multilingualism of Gloria Anzaldúa, whose eight languages range from Standard English to Standard Spanish to Tex-Mex;

Jamaica Kincaid's anger that "the only language I have in which to speak of this crime (of enslavement) is the language of the criminal who committed the crime," which "can explain and express the deed only from the criminal's point of view." Feminist criticism has also raised questions about "women's language" and about the particularly dialogic forms that nonhegemonic writers may adopt to open up or circumvent conventional androcentric languages. In light of these challenges, comparative literature's notions of language have been, like its canon, only narrowly comparative.

It seems plausible to me that one reason why so many of these values have persisted in comparative literature even though similar positions have been dismantled in related disciplines is that institutionally ours remains a beleaguered field, routinely having to justify its existence and its disciplinary integrity. We may feel especially defensive now that theory, once comparative literature's bailiwick, is taught routinely in so many departments of national (and particularly English) literature along with an expanding global curriculum in which works in translation are increasingly routine. It seems to me that challenges to comparative literature often take the form of threats to the field's "virility" not unlike those directed at women's studies: both are deemed deficient in definitive boundaries and methodology, lacking in "rigor" and "precision," professionally impractical. Comparative literature has tended to resist these charges with a manly counterelitism that asserts its superiority to national literary studies on the grounds of a rigorous insistence on the "mastery" of foreign languages and literatures, an engagement with complex Continental theories, a concern with the world's great "monuments," and what Werner Friedrich calls "hard, scholarly principles." A critical aspect of this self-legitimation has been a sometimes vehement dissociation of comparative literature from "general" or "world" literature, which is implied to be an "easy introductory" study of translated works.

But I think there is another, more honorable explanation for the tenacity of the values of universality and transcendence, one that has to do with the political agenda already reflected in early formulations such as those of Goethe and Arnold and especially vigorous when comparative literature was burgeoning earlier in this century. I propose that comparative literature's deep investment in the study of sameness is not only an intellectual agenda but an ideological one, and not only a casualty of cultural solipsism but the unwitting legacy of an urgent need to preserve human dignity and artistic achievement against the real threats of fascism and world war. The investment in sameness is easy to document through decades of apparent dissonance: whether comparative literature has been defined as the study of literature across national boundaries or the study of literature without regard to such boundaries, it has been committed not only intellectually but politically to the notion that literature and aesthetic culture are universal: comparative literature entails "a consciousness of the unity of all literary creation and experience"; "an overall view of literature . . . as inclusive and comprehensive," a focus on "problems that transcend linguistic and national boundaries"; it seeks the "common ground of interest beneath the superficial tangle of differences." François Jost put it most unequivocally in the early 1970s, just when feminist and ethnic studies were emerging in national departments of literature: "The entire globe shares identical literary interests and pursues similar literary goals."

This notion of literature as transcending cultures has an agenda that some comparatists have made explicitly ideological: it is a means for realizing "(our) common humanity"; a way "to consolidate the spiritual unity in our half of the world," a kind of literary United Nations bent on proving the adage that "it's a small world after all." It is therefore appropriate that comparative literature's major tasks as they have traditionally been codified— to study influences and analogies; movements and trends; genres and forms; motifs, types, and themes—encourage us to overlook difference in favor of sameness or to show the essential similarities beneath surface differences, as A. Owen Aldridge does, for example, in treating Natsume Sōseki's *Kokoro* as a "Japanese Werther." Such a project is made immeasurably easier by the persistent white male-centeredness of comparative literature's tools and texts: we are able to define literature, culture, and even "the world" in terms sufficiently narrow to prove our own claims, while sustaining an illusion of breadth by reaching out, like open-minded tourists, to the "finds" among lesser ("folk" and female) cultures and absorbing them into the established museums of literature.

I have said that there were historically progressive reasons why comparative literature developed this universalizing ideology. Comparatism grew up in an era of imperialist nationalism which some comparatists hoped to combat by affirming a transnational spirit in the human sciences. This agenda must have seemed especially pressing in the years when comparative literature was developing in Europe and the United States, since these were years in which the very countries collaborating most fully in the comparative project, France and Germany, were bitter enemies. "Rising above" national boundaries and partisan identities was surely a crucial strategy of resistance, a way to preserve not simply personal and collegial relations, or even the project of comparative literary scholarship, but "culture" itself. It is sadly ironic that this resistance to nationalism ended up constructing an androcentric Continentalism that became its own exclusivity. A sign of the double-talk engendered by such a project may be found in a chilling if well-intentioned passage from Werner Friedrich's 1964 essay "The Challenge of

Comparative Literature." Having proclaimed comparatism to be a "political creed" dedicated to "abjuring all forms of racism"; having lauded the spectrum of European national identities represented among comparatists teaching in the United States (though without mentioning Jews, although several of the men he names are Jewish, and omitting women entirely); having identified the "same inspiring wealth" among "the literary figures of America"; and having unequivocally supported the movement for black civil rights and condemned the violence at Little Rock and Birmingham, Friedrich asks his listeners to consider, "happily and perhaps a bit proudly, that the voice of the Black Man was heard for the first time in history not in Africa, not on the shores of the Congo, but on the shores of the Mississippi—and that it was in ever upward-struggling America that the former slaves . . . were first given a chance to give expression to their hopes and their anguish, to the despair and the vision of a race that is justly aspiring to a respected place on earth." I need not point out the truths of African and American history that are violated in this Eurocentric paean to America for "allowing" black culture to enter its comparative melting pot—as if there had not been centuries of culture in Africa, and as if slavery were now a precondition for literary upward mobility.

Such fictions suggest that comparative literature has embraced "difference" only when it has not visibly entailed dominance, dependence when it has been a matter of indebtedness and not of political power, so that, like Kincaid's tourists, we "needn't let that slightly funny feeling (we) have from time to time about exploitation, oppression, domination develop into full-fledged unease" and ruin not simply our holiday but our livelihood. That comparative literature has preferred not to recognize that "in every cross-cultural encounter there is a dominance, a submission, a merging, or resistance" might explain its particular resistance to feminism, which sees dominance in difference and for which power relations constitute a theoretical core. *A Small Place* is the kind of text that forces issues of power, though comparative analogies with Coleridge, the Bible, or even Swift might temper the book's contemporary urgency. With its direct interrogation of "you," such a book also asks us to acknowledge, as comparatists rarely do, our own cultural differences—hence our relations of dominance, submission, merging, and resistance—with the cultures we "compare." Since the refusal to confront these imbalances of power is, of course, the privilege of the dominant and of those who align themselves with the dominant, the perspective of the "other" (the woman, the person of color, the colonized—the "borderworker") becomes critical for a fully "comparative" view. In *Three Guineas*, Virginia Woolf distinguishes the England of "educated men" ("so kind of you") from her own, women's England ("so harsh to us") and explains

that this is why, "though we look at the same things, we see them differently." This kind of comparative consciousness counters the disciplinary tradition I have been describing in which comparatists look at different things but see them as the same.

I have dwelled at some length on dissonances between feminism and comparatism in order to begin suggesting both a shape and a rationale for a globally conscious feminist comparative literature. Since I began with a polemical statement about comparative literature as it has traditionally been conceptualized, let me move now toward an equally polemical but positive statement about the kind of comparative literature that seems to me most valuable for addressing contemporary concerns such as those *A Small Place* raised for me. Such a comparatism would understand texts as documents whether or not they are monuments and would expand its notions of both "literature" and "theory" to include an international, multiracial, and sexually inclusive spectrum of verbal practices. It would need to redefine nation, culture, and language in broader and more complicated terms, would value difference as least as much as sameness by exploring works in what I will call a comparative specificity, and, in order to resist reinscribing dominance, would locate both its practices and its practitioners within their own cultural space. Such a comparative literature might, I suggest, realize the visions of earlier comparatists from Goethe to Welleck in ways and on grounds they did not imagine, just as the U.S. Constitution makes possible, as Bernice Reagon points out, the freedoms of people whom the "founding fathers" themselves suppressed or enslaved.

First and most obviously, a feminist comparative literature would need to understand literature as document as well as monument, which also means exploring from an international perspective the processes by which certain documents get transformed into monuments and others do not. Such a project would demand an interrogation of comparative literature's tenacious privileging not simply of *an* aesthetic but of *the* aesthetic, an interrogation that feminist criticism initiated in the 1970s and that Barbara Herrnstein Smith and Pierre Bourdieu have theorized in ways that might speak fruitfully to traditionally trained comparatists.

Equally urgent, given the ways in which comparative literature now conceives itself as the locus of "theory," is the need for a revised and expanded notion of that term which embraces not only different theorists and different politics but different *discourses*, including those of people whose primary commitments are not academic but activist and for whom "theory" is manifestly not only about ways to think and read but about ways to live. Such an opening of the theoretical canon would have two crucial results. On the one hand, it would challenge some sacred Eurocentric theoretical

premises. It is clear, for example, that for feminists, for colonized peoples, and for other silenced groups, conceptions of language, truth, and reality often differ from those held by the avant-garde West. When Mary Prince says the "foreign people" who "say slaves are happy" have "put a cloak about the truth," her discourse requires some belief in a recoverable "truth." Similarly, as post-colonialist narratologists such as Mineke Schipper have made clear, "realism" carries different meanings and imperatives for emerging communities, and the preference for realist fiction that has been associated with various liberation movements cannot be dismissed as retrograde. Likewise, William Walsh contrasts the European distrust of language to the Indian view "that immediate experience and its expression in language are not two wholly different things." A genuinely comparative encounter between such different theoretical positions asks those of us trained in "the master's tools" not to dismiss these dissenting voices as "naive" or "untheoretical." Such an encounter may be possible, however, only when comparative literature is willing to read as theory writings that lie outside its canon of philosophy. To the extent that such a canon represents the thought pattens of a ruling-class minority, we must also entertain the possibility that it reinforces the hegemony of the groups that created it, even when the individual theorist (like the individual comparatist) remains "detached" from matters explicitly political.

On the other hand, different theories and theories in different discourses may also intersect fruitfully. I have found significant similarities (along with equally important differences) between some radical theory by women of color and some poststructuralist theory by whites. I am struck, for example, by resonances between Audre Lorde's conception of the relation between poetry and theory in "Poetry Is Not a Luxury" and Julia Kristeva's conception of the relation between the semiotic and the symbolic in *Revolution in Poetic Language*. But Kristeva's is the writing that is counted as theory; as bell hooks notes, current academic practice admits black women to the creative canon but not to the theoretical one, possibly because black women's theories often raise urgent political issues unbuffered by a generalizing academic terminology. If Terry Eagleton is right to say that training in literary studies is training in the ability to manipulate a certain discourse, and that academics are "allowed" to say anything we wish in this discourse because certain things simply cannot be said in it, then the encounter of theories that I am proposing is possible only if we engage in difference in discourse and not simply a difference in "view." Since comparative literature has been avant-garde in taking up (and producing) "theory," it would be appropriate for us now to take a similar role of leadership in expanding the range of our theoretical competence.

Encounters with antimonumental theories and texts will help—or require—us to redefine nation, culture, and language in new terms. Woolf's contrasts between "male" and "female" England and Kincaid's among Antiguan classes and races make clear the need not to rely on assumptions about national or cultural unity but to confront as subjects of comparison differences within nations and cultures—the differences of race, sex, ethnicity, religion, sexuality, region, and class that in fact get repressed when nations and cultures define themselves." We can also study the comparative intersection of various differences, as Selma James does when she looks through Sir Thomas Bertram's role as a(n Antiguan) slaveholder at his governance of Mansfield Park. In this process James shows the value of gender difference to cultural study: "The effect of dismissing as unimportant what Jane Austen says women of the slaveholding class had to bear at the hands of the master is to dismiss the attack on the slaveholder that comes from within his family."

Such studies suggest the need for a revision of both the concept and the place of language in comparative literature. We might begin by recognizing that languages embed relations of dominance, as François de Grafigny already understood in 1747 when she accused the French of "according merit to other countries to the extent that their manners imitate our own and their language resembles our idiom." We might then want to "compare" intralingual differences such as dialect and register, or different literatures (Afro-Caribbean and African American, or African American and Jewish American) within the "same" language group. We must also make the crucial distinctions between language and culture that allow comparison, for example, of anglophone African and Indian women writers, or anglophone and Tamil Indian writers, or Jamaica Kincaid's *Annie John* and Annie's "favorite" novel, *Jane Eyre*. In Bharati Mukherjee's *Jasmine* (1989), an Iowan asks the narrator to "come up with a prettier name"—"something in Indian"—for the golf course he imagines building on the family farm. The narrator comments: "I want to say to Darrel, 'You mean in Hindi, not Indian, there's no such thing as Indian,' but . . . he comes from a place where the language you speak is what you are." This passage suggests the importance of distinguishing cultural from linguistic training and creating a comparative literature that embraces both. This does not mean abandoning "foreign language" requirements; on the contrary, at this moment when linguistic imperialism is rising and the study of languages remains in decline, one valuable task the discipline could undertake is to enable students to learn under-studied languages, languages that are primarily oral, and languages of newly literate cultures so that such writings can become part of a fully global literature. This project, in turn, will create a future

community of scholars whose linguistic base is immeasurably broader than that of my generation of comparatists.

Such a linguistic reformation would facilitate a deconstruction of the political and cultural hierarchies which, in its efforts at transcendence, comparative literature has tended to reproduce. We would be avoiding what John Dorsey calls a "cultural wealth-of-nations outlook," the position whereby the "best" literatures, or those most worth studying are those with the most exports. (Feminist criticism, my own work by no means excepted, has already reproduced such dominance in its overconcentration on British, French, and U.S. works.) This means resisting a superpower comparatism by which smaller literatures (including literature by women) are overlooked by or swallowed up in larger ones. In fact, one fertile field for comparative study is precisely the relationship between the production (and reception) of literature and various forms of global power—political, linguistic, economic, cultural. Comparative literature could help to rebalance the cultural map by studying the literal and metaphoric "small places" we have traditionally overlooked. If we value linguistic difference and richness, then let us follow Albert Wendt's call to explore the literatures of Oceania, with its 1,200 indigenous languages in addition to English, French, Hindi, Spanish, and various forms of pidgin, which give this region, Wendt argues, a potential to be the most creative in the world. Let us explore complex relations between gender and colonialism which Edna Manlapaz queries, for example, when she explains that it was the overthrow of Spanish imperialism in the Philippines by its American counterpart that gave Philippine women the equivocal gift of a university education to write literature in a foreign tongue within a British-American intertext. And let us acknowledge that much of the globe—including Europe—is becoming what Ulf Hannerz calls "creolized," so that even to speak of individual nations or continents, or "East" and "West," is becoming culturally inaccurate.

A new comparative practice might also entail redefining or replacing those traditional modes for organizing literary study which have encouraged homogeneity. Joan Kelly's now classic argument that women did not have a Renaissance reminds us that most literary periodizations suit only the productions of European men. Kincaid writes that "to the people in a small place, the division of Time into the Past, the Present, and the Future does not exist." Women have likewise written about gendered differences in understandings of time. It may become more fruitful to supplement the notion of chronological period by identifying movements or impulses that occur at different times in different places but have similar consequences, so that, for example, one might identify moments in which there seems to be an insertion of anticolonialism or feminism into a culture's discourses. Genre

theory would likewise need deconstruction, given the ways in which marginalized literatures have either been omitted from genre studies or have themselves rejected conventional generic forms. And "influence" would surely have to be redefined to account for the nonsalutary as well as the benevolent: the influence of England on Antigua, the related influence of *Jane Eyre* or *The Tempest* on Caribbean writers, the subtler influences of hegemonies (male, white, European) that "outsider" writers have both accommodated and resisted in complex ways. Obviously, notions of "tradition" would have to be revised as we interrogate the restrictive and selective uses to which the concept has been put and the values and agendas served by the legitimation that the word provides.

All these practices imply a conception of the comparative that is grounded in the assumption of difference as a premise at least equal to the assumption of similarity. Such a position opens infinitely more complicated ways to understand textual relations as racial, sexual, regional, or colonial and to recognize that a considerable share of the world's literature is "borderwork." Those of us trained as traditional comparatists would have to resist our easy reach for the similar. Now that I have learned, for example, that Kincaid acknowledges Alain Robbe-Grillet to be a major influence, I would have to temper my wish to turn her uses of the you-as-protagonist into a simple replication of *nouveau roman* strategies.

The key to such a revised practice seems to me to lie in the idea of what I call a *comparative specificity*, which would embrace both difference and similarity but would never simply dissolve a text, idea, writer, group, or movement into a safe and homogeneous whole. Angelika Bammer's study of feminism and utopianism in the 1970s models such specificity by understanding feminism as a multinational movement of nationally situated politics. What happens when such understanding is absent is dramatically illustrated in Kelly Cherry's review of *A Small Place*, which lambastes Kincaid's book precisely for its specificity:

> It is not that the author is wrong to be so furious but that she truncates the reader's sympathy for her emotion by denying . . . that there are other sources of rage, rage as deep as hers.
> . . . Every one of us *is* an island, "a small place" harboring the humiliations and despairs of a history of abuse, racial or sexual, political or economic, personal or professional.

When Cherry turns Kincaid's "small place' into a metaphor, she erases the particular pain of slavery and colonialist racism beneath a fiction of universal and presumably equal suffering. Isabelle de Charrière's *Lettres ècrites de*

Lausanne (1785) enacts a similar universalizing gesture when Cècile finds herself pitying a "poor Negro" sold into slavery and now dying alone in Geneva, but then "corrects" herself by commenting that it doesn't really matter whether one is a slave or a king since both will die: "The King of France will be like this slave one day." I am suggesting that comparative literature at this historical moment needs to allow the slave a specificity that is dissolved in this analogy with the King of France as in the metaphorizing of Antigua as an island of generic pain. The slave narrator Mary Prince reveals the danger of such idealist slippages when she talks of Christianity's messages to slaves that "the truth will make me free" when in fact it was not "the truth" but white colonizers who had that power.

Finally, a global feminist comparative literature would have to acknowledge that comparatists are individuals constituted in culture—in nation, gender, class, race, ethnicity, religion, ideology, sexuality. To "compare" would mean neither a denial of these specificities nor an imprisonment within them, but a dialectical engagement of what Adrienne Rich calls a "politics of location" with what Virginia Woolf calls a "freedom from unreal loyalties" which together would allow one—paradoxically and probably always only partially—to stand "outside" the very culture in which one also locates oneself and one's work. We would first need to accept Rich's recognition that "as a woman (comparatist) I have a country; as a woman (comparatist) I cannot divest myself of that country merely by condemning its government (or by styling myself a "world citizen"). Although comparatists may not live in our culture of origin, none of us is a culture-free globe dweller, and most are white, European, and middle-class in ethnic origin, training, or outlook. We have proceeded as if these identities, and the differences both among ourselves and between ourselves and the cultures we are studying, did not exist. Comparative literature has, in effect, echoed Virginia Woolf's claim that "as a woman I have no country. As a woman I want no country. As a woman my country is the whole world" without recognizing as Woolf did the need first to divest oneself of one's "unreal loyalties," the seductions that stem from "pride of nationality . . . religious pride, college pride, school pride, family pride, sex pride" in order to see from a critical comparative vantage point.

Indeed, Woolf's strategy for achieving this balance between location and distance was precisely through comparative studies; she asked her woman reader to "compar(e) French historians with English; German with French; the testimony of the ruled—the Indians or the Irish, say—with the claims made by their rulers," and then if there remained "some 'patriotic' emotion, some ingrained belief in the intellectual superiority of her own country over other countries," to "compare English painting with French painting; English music with German music; English literature with Greek literature; for translations abound. When all these comparisons have been faithfully made by the use of reason, the outsider will find herself in possession of very good reasons for her indifference." Woolf's suggestion that women and other outsiders might have a particular critical perspective on their "own" culture seems to me amply supported by the revision I have been engaging here, which was made possible by the thinking of women such as Woolf and Rich, Lorde and Kincaid, Mukherjee and Grafigny, who refuse to engage in "unreal loyalties" yet who locate their own comparative practices within the framework of their sex, race, sexuality, and nationality instead of pretending to proceed, as the 1979 ICLA (International Comparative Literature Association) defined the comparative project, from "an international point of view."

I conclude with the utopian suggestion that this kind of specific and located cross-cultural comparative practice might help to fulfill the desires of the earlier comparatists for a just and harmonious world, goals that I believe can be achieved not by denying relations of power and difference but only by confronting and dismantling them. Comparative literature's future may well lie in those texts it has ignored and marginalized and in a new generation of scholars from around the world who will take the discipline, as *A Small Place* has taken me, into the places of discomfort that are so often the places of growth.

H. ADLAI MURDOCH

Severing the (M)Other Connection: The Representation of Cultural Identity in Jamaica Kincaid's Annie John

One of the most intricate questions dealt with by the Caribbean writer in recent years has been that of identity. The issue of subjectivity, beset with problems such as recognition of self and other and oedipal conflict under the most conventional circumstances, is complicated further here given the additional factors of colonialism and pluralism which continue to mark Caribbean society and culture. One recent work which tackles such questions is Jamaica Kincaid's *Annie John*. Set in the Antigua of the 1950s, this autobiographic novel recounts a succession of experiences which culminate in the protagonist's almost palpable hatred for her mother. Underlying its apparent linearity, however, are various tropes and figures which trace Annie's desire to establish an individual identity within the complexities of Caribbean social structure. The specific psychoanalytical concepts which bear upon and explicate her wish for separation will be shown at several points to be impacted not only by the exigencies of Caribbean history, but by its racial pluralities as well.

The quest for identity in which the protagonist engages in this novel is mediated primarily by the Lacanian paradigm of the alienated subject. Lacan himself posits this alienation by delineating clearly the split inherent in subjectivity: "Identity is realized as disjunctive of the subject . . . since it is the subject who introduces division into the individual, as well as into the collectivity that is his equivalent." In her exemplary work entitled *Jacques*

From *Callaloo* 13:2., Spring 1990. © 1990 by The Johns Hopkins University Press.

Lacan, Anika Lemaire says of this split subject that "the truth about himself, which language fails to provide him with, will be sought in images of others with whom he will identify." In this case the protagonist, unable to achieve assonance with the world around her, identifies with the image of the other in the form of her mother in an effort to establish a coherent self. This symbiotic relationship appears to function until the falseness of its premise is exposed to her, an event which is specifically precipitated by a primal scene. This, in turn, gives rise to a new perception of the mother as being both racially and culturally different. The mother's creole Dominican past becomes opposed to Annie's Antiguan cultural formation, so that the mother's cultural separateness and "foreignness" are interpreted as a form of racial difference. This ideal of racial difference as a subset of "foreignness" thus initially terminates the primary state in which Annie seeks her identity through the (m)other. In conjunction with the primal scene, it also gives rise to Annie's perception of her mother's abdication of authority, precipitating her rejection of that unique sense of unity that had bound them together.

It is subsequent to the illumination conveyed by this episode that Annie's rebellion, malevolence, and hatred of her mother will develop. Her eventual departure from her homeland is the outcome of her recognition of an existence which she has outgrown and a step toward the establishment of a newer, more valid one. The concepts of racial difference and identity thus assume a very particular form in this text, one directly influenced by the structure and relationships of the West Indian family, as well as by the racial and cultural admixture of the Caribbean region. It is the problematic of establishing a valid identity within this context, subject all the while to pressures of alienation, race, gender, and culture, that makes Annie John's case unique, and makes these factors our specific points of analytical reference.

In terms of genre, *Annie John* must be classified as a *Bildungsroman*, or novel of coming of age, of discovery of self, which recounts the process of growing up and coming to terms with the world. Conventions of reading lead us to posit the treatment of the protagonist's physical and spiritual development within this genre, leading to the destruction of illusion and the acquisition of maturity. It is in these terms that the literary world has recognized and codified masterworks by such European authors as Joyce, Proust, and Flaubert. We may say, at the outset, that the treatment of content and theme makes *Annie John* a part of this tradition, although in a rather specialized way: the concatenation of sex and race, geography and culture, tends to cause the novel to diverge somewhat from the white, male, European tradition of the *Bildungsroman*. Not only is the novel the product of an author who differs from this tradition in terms of sex, race, and culture, but the ontological basis of the protagonist's struggle is itself couched in terms of the establishment of a self which will draw its validity and its motivation for being from a vision of difference based, at least in part, on perceptions of gender, race, and culture. As such, the very discourse of the novel—specifically the genesis of identity as it is addressed here—derives from and speaks to a particular cultural milieu whose conditions of existence determine, in their turn, the way in which signification is constructed in the novel. This particularity of culture also serves to differentiate the novel from the canon of Afro-American women's fiction, for considerations of history, social structure, geography, and culture suggest that such canonization represents a misreading of crucial elements of the text. As was indicated above, the exigencies of Caribbean culture are of a very specific nature, and it is to this cultural milieu that we must now turn.

There is a large cultural and historical matrix which particularizes the experience of the inhabitants of the region. The islands of the Eastern Caribbean, most of which are former slave colonies of Great Britain, are made up of remnants of previous slave societies, and thus always have had populations that are mainly black in most cases, but which are quite mixed in some others. In *Slavery and Social Death*, Orlando Patterson points out that, even as far back as 1708, Antigua's slave population numbered 12,943, while the white population was 2,909; by 1834, the slave population had risen to 29,100, while the white population stood at 2,000. Further, Antigua was the only one of the Caribbean islands whose slaves were not subjected to a "trial period" of "freedom apprenticeship," lasting four years, following Emancipation on 1 August 1834, in a caveat which elsewhere would become slavery in all but name. In Antigua, however, freedom was immediate and total; free villages were established, rejoicing in the resonant symbolism of names such as Freetown, Liberta, and Freeman'sville, and blacks became independent wage-earners with the option, if deemed necessary or justified, of withholding their labor where and when they saw fit. In some other islands, however, populations became quite mixed, and considerations of topography and biculturalism took them down quite different developmental paths.

It is the differential traced by the results of both these developmental paradigms that helps determine the eventual perception of the mother's difference by her daughter. Blackness and the black population became the racial and ontological norm in some islands, but this was not always the case, and this factor will be of primary importance when looking at the question of identity formation. For this is also the question that goes to the heart of Annie's eventual perception of her mother's "difference." Annie's mother is of Dominican parentage; she migrated to Antigua at age sixteen and, we are told, barely survived the trip due to a hurricane. It is at this juncture that issues of colonial history come to bear upon the twentieth century Caribbean sense of self. Antigua's history as a British colony shows that, subsequent to colonization in 1632, the British relinquished possession of the island for only a very short period in the mid-nineteenth century. Dominica, on the other hand, was one of those territories whose history and culture is marked by extended possession and influence by the French during this period, before being annexed by the British in 1783. The legacies of such colonial domination inhere in the persistence of cultural differences within the island chain, differences whose most immediate result has been to perpetuate perceptions of intra-regional insularity, especially in the domains of language and racial appearance as markers of cultural identity.

As far as language is concerned, for example, whereas the structure of Antiguan dialect is based, at least in part, on English and African language forms, the Dominican dialect is French and African-based, and the island is in fact closer, linguistically, culturally, and geographically, to the French Departments of Guadeloupe and Martinique than to those territories subjected to British influence. People from separate islands, in fact, tend to see each other as being "different," and this seems an unalterable feature of West Indian culture. Indeed, the very racial structure of the territories varies as well, with those of French background demonstrating the results of a more thorough-going racial admixture. By putting Annie's Dominican mother into place as a creole "metis," or mixed, woman, then, one who incorporates a certain "difference" in terms of appearance and language, these secondary characteristics become the ones which are jolted to the forefront of Annie's perception as part of the recognition process in the primal scene. Her mother, as we shall see, becomes "foreign" to her on a plural level, one which joins the issues of race and culture to the creation of identity. But before exploring this question, let us turn, briefly, to another context signified by and necessary to this text; that of feminine oedipal paradigm.

On the face of it, the narrative of *Annie John* and the mother/daughter relationship do not demand analysis exclusively through the prism of the feminine oedipus. There are, however, certain elements of the narrative structure which suggest the possible efficacy of a reading of this kind. First among these are the character relationships, especially among the three primary participants, Annie and her parents. An explanation of the Freudian oedipal paradigm may provide some grounds for reading from such a perspective.

The Freudian paradigm of the feminine oedipus is derived essentially from Freud's general oedipal theory. In both cases, emphasis is laid on the function of the castration complex. The well-known formula of the male oedipus has the boy wanting to kill off his father and sleep with his mother, a desire to which the father puts an end by asserting his power over and

possession of the mother, effectively castrating the boy. In the feminine paradigm, the girl blames her mother for the state of castration that she perceives
in them both during the phallic phase, and denigrates her mother at the same
time for having succumbed to a phallic power greater than that of the clitoris.
It is at this point that the father, the repository of greater phallic power,
becomes the focal point of the girl's predilections, the mother's submission
being seen as a sort of betrayal.

There is another explanation for the girl's turn to the father, one
favored by object-relations theorists, and elaborated by Nancy Chodorow in
The Reproduction of Mothering. Here, an all-powerful mother fulfills the role
of castrator, and the turning to the father is seen as a means of liberation
from the all-subsuming female, a way for the girl to establish a separate feminine self. We will argue that it is the attempt at separation and differentiation from the mother, as well as the perception of maternal castration as
viewed in and stemming from the primal scene, that initiate Annie John's
rebellion against her mother. But to do this, we must first look more closely
at the nature of the West Indian family, whose paradoxical form has implications not only for Annie's recognition of and identification with a maternal
power structure, but for the particular operation here of the feminine oedipal
paradigm as well.

Now, there should be no question as to the general validity of
describing the West Indies as a male-dominated culture. In her study of
family structures and relationships, *My Mother Who Fathered Me,* which uses
Jamaica as the sociological crucible of the Caribbean, Edith Clarke points
out that West Indian men enjoy much greater social and sexual freedom than
do West Indian women. They are the focus of society's power relationships
and occupy, in general, positions within it which inculcate concomitant attitudes of social and psychological authority. They maintain sometimes
numerous and contemporaneous extra-familial sexual relationships, a luxury
that women certainly are not afforded by them. Theirs is also the major share
of responsibility in financial maintenance of the household, and upkeep of
the children in or out of wedlock, although this may be the ideal rather than
the reality. West Indian men, in other words, are allowed by society to
indulge in libidinal pleasures; tacit recognition is given to their overwhelmingly dominant role in all social relationships.

However, this paradigm of male dominance overlooks a paradox crucial
not only to filial relationships within the society at large, but to Annie's relationship to her mother in particular. Here is Edith Clarke once again:
"mother and children co-operate in the small daily duties in the home. They
are continually together. . . . Whatever she may be doing in the yard, the
children are never very far away. There is constant companionship, and *a*

constant interdependence. The girl child identifies herself with the mother." This matriarchal structure is the locus of the power with which Annie identifies, and which sets up the groundwork for the oedipal paradigm to function as a means of maternal separation within the Caribbean cultural context. In other words, the tendency of the girl to seek identity through the (m)other, valorizing this relationship as it occurs within the cultural and domestic domains, will elicit rebellion when such a symbiosis is perceived as being betrayed. This will be the ultimate result of Annie's incursion into the primal scene; the repudiation of the mother and the turn toward the father both are determined culturally, as well as psychologically. Further, as Maria Ramas points out, if "the notion of an omnipotent mother seeking to prevent her child's individuation has a material basis," lending a "certain plausibility to the suggestion that the girl views the father as a potential liberator," it should not be surprising that these structures are reflected in the narrative, a situation which, as we shall see, is certainly the case. Finally, having established the matriarchal nature of West Indian family structure, then Ramas's further point, that "the dyadic structure (mother/child) [is] the elemental relational structure within which gender identify and sexuality are formed," becomes the basis for the filial conflict which is acted out in the pages of *Annie John.* As we shall see, the relationship bears the marks not only of the feminine oedipus, but also for the Lacanian Imaginary, a concept which will be examined in due course. But now we finally are able to initiate the first stage of our textual analysis.

Not only is death closely associated with many of the leading characters in *Annie John*, but the novel, for all practical purposes, opens onto the cemetery. The figure of the undertaker, and the death of Annie's young friend, Nalda, serve to fix the importance to be attached to tropes of death in the minds of both Annie and the reader. Great literary value also is attached to the figure of the mother, as early on in the novel she is the locus of two literary figures: her involvement in the deaths of both Nalda and Miss Charlotte prefigures certain facets of her eventual conflict with Annie; and the synechdoche of the mother's hands is also a harbinger of its eventual repetition in the primal scene. But we are getting ahead of ourselves. Also worthy of note is Annie's emphasis on funerals, their organization and her attendance at them. When the humpbacked girl of her own age dies, Annie's responses border on the grotesque. She wishes she had tapped the dead girl's hump to see if it was hollow, compares her death pallor to the way a scene might appear through a malfunctioning View-Master, and expresses the fear that the dead girl would return and ask Annie's father to make her, Annie, a coffin. These responses may be taken as being representative of Annie's thought. She clearly does not share the usual thought-processes or imaginative scenarios of others, and this alienation will make itself more and more apparent in her behavior as the narrative progresses. By the time the first chapter ends, Annie has been caught in a first lie, brought on by her obsession with death and funerals. When combined with the account of the sadistic aspects of her relationships with her friend Sonia, whose mother dies, we have in place arguably the first sign of that combination of evil and rebellion through which she is projected at the center of the narrative.

The closeness of Annie to her mother, the extent to which she identifies with the maternal image, is valorized in fact through their mutual participation in things like the ritualized baths, where the description of *obeah* practices—*obeah* being the Antiguan term for a local form of "voudoun"— provides an element of added realism beyond the purely geographical. This closeness is elaborated upon further by Annie's description of her initiation into the domestic world of the period: "I spent the day following my mother around and observing the way she did everything." She states how important she felt to be with her mother and, beyond the culinary realism of describing local dishes and ingredients, indicates that her mother simply wanted to "include (her) in everything." Finally, here, Annie's description of her mother begins by equating her beauty and her daughter's feelings for her with those of a queen, whose head would in fact have been on the sixpence to which she refers. This is in direct contrast to her almost throwaway description of her father's looks and how she felt about them, and, to some extent, him at that time: "When my eyes rested on my father, I didn't think very much of the way he looked. But when my eyes rested on my mother, I found her beautiful." Now, what is most striking about this comparison is that it has the effect of creating an emphatic reinforcement of Annie's attachment to an identification with her mother in the mind of the reader. It also demonstrates the narrative value of the mother as well as the secondary value which both narrative and protagonist attach to the father, a hierarchy which also will progressively change. In other words, Annie's tendency to seek her identity through the image of the (m)other, as well as possibilities for eventual racial and oedipal differentiation, are already in place at this juncture. There can be no doubt, then, of the extent to which Annie John identifies with and valorizes the maternal image at this stage: no overt hint of the approaching struggle to achieve a separate identity. But the clouds on the horizons are figured in different ways, and here they will create a narrative threat which, unraveling progressively throughout the text, succeeds in deconstructing the apparently idyllic existence that a first impression would tend to affirm.

The protagonist next proceeds to restate, and thus to revalorize in the economy of the text, the association of her mother with tropes of death by describing her mother's emigratory boat trip from Dominica to Antigua, during which the boat encountered a hurricane and several people drowned. The reference is thus not only prefigurative in the subsequent perception of the mother's "foreignness," and the reversal of attachments that will proceed from it, but by putting the mother's departure into place as an integral stage in the development of one with whom she identifies, it will allow Annie eventually to repeat this departure in her turn, in order to achieve her own identity. But for the moment, the narrative leads us to consider in greater detail one particular item, the mother's trunk.

The significance of Annie's mother's trunk cannot be overstated. It eventually will assume primary importance in the text as an indicator of repression and discontent. Here are stored garments and other markers of Annie's infancy, as well as certificates of merit and other objects associated with, tracing, and representing Annie's life. The trunk and its contents will assume their function later in the text, in an excellent use of narrative deferral, as representations of Annie's fragmented self and her need for self-identity and self-expression; they are put into place here as a symbolic depiction of Annie herself, and thus of the mother's enclosure, containment, limitation, possession and direction of her daughter's life and identity. This *topos* of unnaming, of reification and reduction of the protagonist, is given further import by the mother's practice of recounting to Annie stories of her life which seem themselves to be buried in the trunk along with these objects, and gives additional credence to a certain superiority and control on the part of the mother, based on knowledge which she alone, of the two, possesses.

Further complicating this situation is the fact that both mother and daughter have identical names: Annie John bears exactly the same name as her mother, Annie John. By and large, there is nothing intrinsically wrong with such an arrangement. But when it is combined with the behavioral and psychological factors which have been delineated above, one must conclude that we are being presented with a vision of an omnipotent, all-subsuming mother—a phallic mother, if you will, a figure generated by this particular Caribbean family structure—who holds ultimate power both in the family hierarchy in general and over her daughter in particular. In this regard, Julia Kristeva has described this maternal phenomenon in "Stabat Mater" "embod(ying) an absolute authority the more attractive as it appeared removed from paternal sternness . . . but no less authoritarian, the underhand double of explicit phallic power." This phallic construct goes hand in hand with the matriarchal family structure, valorizing the mother in the eyes of Annie and generating the identification and authority with which she identifies and which determine both her present and her future. In this context, the placement of the objects in the mother's trunk, in conjunction with that prized filial bond and the coincidence of names, point to an almost total assimilation of one Annie by the other—the enclosure and erasure on the part of the mother of any attempt by her daughter to lead an independent existence in whatever form. In other words, Annie's ability to recognize herself as a subject is circumscribed severely; in seeking the truth of herself through the image of the (m)other, with whom she identifies, she is alienated both from herself and from the world around her. Her inability to perceive this alienation will render the break between them that much more inevitable and agonizing.

Annie therefore is left with a structured self whose particular elements—especially the tendency to recognize the self in and through images of the other—may be defined as being characteristic of the mirror state of the Lacanian Imaginary:

> This self-recognition is . . . a mis-recognition; the subject apprehends itself only by means of a fictional construct whose defining characteristics—focus, coordination—it does not share. It must also be stressed that the mirror stage is one of those crises of alienation around which the Lacanian subject is organized, *since to know oneself through an external image is to be defined through self-alienation.*

It is by exposing the false nature of this external image that Annie eventually will recognize the need for separation and individual identity. Her involvement in the primal scene will illuminate a clash of race and culture between herself and her mother, elements heretofore perceived in terms of indivisibility and homogeneity.

Self-alienation, in other words, is the ultimate sign of this stage of Annie's life. It accounts for anomalies in her behavior and thought patterns, and—although she is as yet unaware of it—provides an explanation for her fascination with death and death images. But this obsession is not an end unto itself; it is, in its turn, a literary and psychological manifestation of something else: a sign, in the endless regeneration and plethora of signs, of the inhibitions and identity—repression to which Annie is subject. In other words, the morbidity which seems to lurk around the friends and family of Annie John is a tropological indication of her twin desires for escape and rebellion. We see that her father also becomes a part of these associations, the account of his journey to manhood—involving the disappearance of his own parents and his waking up beside his dead grandmother—paralleling the association of the mother with tropes of death and repression. In Annie's eyes, both parents have become repressive, these instances of disappearance and death prefiguring *topoi* which later will assume tremendous significance in the matrix of the narrative.

It must be stressed, however, that these signs are manifested in spite of Annie's unawareness and ignorance of their meaning. Conscious knowledge of the significance of the relationship with her mother eventually will occur only in the primal scene; but Annie does receive a first inkling of it shortly before this. As she enters puberty, her mother decides to terminate the practice of having both their dresses cut from the same material, which had encouraged the perception of even physical identity between the two: "It's time you had your own clothes. You just cannot go around the rest of your life looking like a little me." Now, whether the mother's original intent was to be omnipotent to the point of projection of physical identity between herself and her daughter cannot be inferred with certainty. In any case, it seems fair to say that Annie interprets this gestures as a form of abandonment: "To say that I felt the earth swept away from under me would not be going too far . . . I was . . . feeling bitterness and hatred, directed not so much toward my mother as toward, I suppose, life in general." For replication of the image of the other, in which mimetic illusion is mistaken for reality, was the only existence Annie knew, and, mis-recognition aside, this existence was being denied her. But it is the subsequent incident that provides her, at last, with true and proper perspective.

One Sunday afternoon, Annie returns home unannounced and, unknown to them, witnesses her parents making love. This is a vision that signifies a major turning point, both psychologically and narratologically, in the chain of events. First, this event constitutes what is known in psychological terms as the "primal scene," a term defined in *The Language of Psychoanalysis* as the "scene of sexual intercourse between the parents which the child observes. . . . It is generally interpreted by the child as an act of violence on the part of the father." Now, already having made the point that West Indian society is a matriarchal one, it is important to emphasize here that the mother is thus usually the wielder of ultimate authority within the structure of the family. Edith Clarke clearly establishes that the mother assumes primary responsibility for familial discipline and instruction: "The training of children in the home devolves largely on the mother . . . In all aspects of home training the mother is the principal actor. The child's most intimate relationship in the home is with her even in those cases where the father is present and associates himself with the upbringing of the child." We already have established that the mother's position within the family hierarchy makes her in effect a phallic mother, the ultimate repository and embodiment, vis-à-vis Annie, of power and authority. When these facts are coupled with the attribution to the father of violence during the sexual act, we may posit certain conclusions.

The attribution of violence, itself a recognition of capacity for power, may be linked to sexual position; the male-superior position, which is the case here—or in fact any position which allows a physically superior participant—may be made to bear the imputation of prepotence, activity, and power, while the person beneath will be seen as passive, powerless, and inferior. Thus what Annie perceives is a massive, unconscionable, and inexplicable loss of power on the part of her mother—one amounting to a betrayal—as the sole means of accounting for her succumbing to the greater physical and phallic power of the father. Such a perceived abandonment of power will engender revision of the appropriateness of fusion with the image of the (m)other, causing Annie to rebel in revenge for having been deserted. More importantly, perhaps, the scene also conveys the recognition of the mother's racial difference, linking race, culture, oedipus, and identity in a single, specific, polyvalent signifier.

This idea is borne out by the now-repeated synechdoche of the mother's hands—"Her hand! It was *white* and bony as if it had *long been dead* and had been left out in the elements. It seemed not to be her hand, yet it could only be her hand, so well did I know it" (emphasis added). The hand is a sign—signifying recognition of loss, betrayal, and alienation, exacerbated by the circling motion indicative of pleasure, and adding insult to injury. Its apparent earlier demise signifies the culmination of images associated with death, linked here to the betrayal now attributed to the mother to create the representation of the mother's symbolic death. Yet its "whiteness" also signifies Annie's contextualization of newly-recognized but previously unimportant factors.

Her mother is not doubly different to her, the creole element in her appearance and language, previously unimportant and unobtrusive, now taking on a negative significance. The idea of racial difference, in the specific form that it assumes in these islands as the result of colonial history and a historically imposed separation of peoples, is uppermost in the perception of difference that accompanies Annie's sense of betrayal. The tendency for Caribbean people to see those from other islands as "different"—whether due to skin tone, hair texture, inflection and vocabulary, or a simple difference in language—surfaces here in conjunction with the oedipal paradigm to particularize this traumatic event. The "beautiful long neck" and the "long plaited hair . . . pinned up around the crown of her head," signs of beauty at an earlier point in the narrative, now reflect a heritage and culture which are "foreign" to Annie's Antigua-based experience. There would have to be a point in her development where Annie would perceive her mis-recognition for what it was and realize what it had cost her. The fact that her perception takes this form may be explained by the Caribbean subject's subordination to historical and cultural forces beyond her control and, usually, her awareness. Yet, paradoxically, difference is at the service of identity here. For the mother's difference must be recognized and rebelled against if Annie is to have an *Antiguan* identity of her own. When, in its turn, this identity becomes insufficient, Annie will leave Antigua for England, replacing her mother with the colonial "mother country." The duality of her alienation at this point is crucial to both her own development and to that of the narrative itself.

So there can be no question that Annie's perception of her mother has undergone a radical change. She now sees herself as betrayed, and assumes, in turn, a potion of power within the mother/daughter hierarchy, signified by the act of talking back to her mother for the first time: "I had never talked back to her before . . . . From the back, she looked small and funny. . . . I was sure I could never let those hands touch me again; I was sure I could never let her kiss me again. All that was finished." Subsequent efforts on Annie's part will be aimed at distance and divorce from that mother who betrayed them both, revealed the hitherto unseen creole side of herself, and is seen now as unworthy; instead, she will attach herself to her father, whose image, in spite of his perceived violent streak, would be seen now as less impersonal and distant, more tempered, more valorized, and a more worthwhile and dependable repository of power, in her eyes.

The autobiographical essay written on her first day at her new school constitutes an embedded narrative, an event where "one sequence is inserted into another as specification or detailing of its functions." In this sequence, Annie recounts having gone swimming with her mother, the mother's apparent disappearance, her reappearance on a distant rock, and her extended obliviousness to Annie's frantic attempts to attract her attention. She goes on to tell of subsequently having experienced the scenario several times in a dream, in which her mother, now joined by Annie's father, never came back. This is simply one of several varieties of embedding short narratives within a main narrative; the case we are dealing with here may be defined as a "relation of thematic juxtaposition . . . examples or stories that form a contrast with the preceding one." We may also describe the function of this embedding as placing in sharper focus the content and theme of the main narrative; through the specific contextual rewriting of tropes and figures already at work in the main text, it may be seen as a contrasted representation of the *topoi* already circulating in Annie's mind: separation, the disappearance of loved ones and the haunting persistence of death images. But the second part of this embedded narrative purports to be a dream, which allows the return and repetition of the *topoi* of the first part, which in their turn repeat those of the main text. This sort of narrative sequencing may be elucidated by a few words from Peter Brooks:

> Repetition in the text is a return, a calling back or a turning back . . . both returns to and returns of . . . returns to origins and returns of the repressed . . . we cannot really move ahead until we have understood that still enigmatic past, yet, ever . . . forward, since revelation, tied to the past, belongs to the future.

Repression, the key link between past, present, and future, figures both narrative and protagonist through a web of signification that becomes increasingly more complex. As we shall see, the repetition-compulsion associated with the repression will surface at the end of the narrative with Annie's repetition of her mother's departure from Dominica, complete with trunk, thus generating Annie's future out of her mother's past while still establishing a specific, different identity.

The double form of this embedded narrative thus will demand a two-part analysis. First, Annie's fears of loss and of separation from her mother as they have been portrayed here are representations of repressed anxieties: the mother as the locus of difference, as the element of the dyad whose skin is lighter and who is "foreign," causes the fear and novelty of separation to emerge as haunting figures. Surfacing once again in this form, the repression and its subject clearly signify key aspects of Annie's past and future. Second, the dream sequence can been seen in terms of unconscious desire. In *The Interpretation of Dreams*, Freud assimilates the dream-content to wish-fulfillment: "as we are told by dream-interpretation, a dream represents a fulfilled wish." Elizabeth Wright glosses this definition further by pointing out that "the energizing force of dreams springs from an unconscious impulse seeking fulfillment, a desire not fulfilled in waking life." It is therefore clear that one possible conclusion to be drawn here—if we accept the dictum that a dream is the disguised fulfillment of a repressed wish—is that Annie's dream vision of her mother oblivious to her on the rock in the sea represents an unconscious desire for separation from the mother, in patent opposition to the overt content of the preceding narrative sequence. It also seems clear that the mother's reaction to this narrative—"a turned back and a warning"—is in fact to the reality of the situation, thus establishing a correlation between recent events and the unconscious desire manifest in the dream sequence.

Annie's growing love for Gwen, which is recounted in the latter half of Chapter Three, accomplishes two things—it replaces one female object of adoration, the mother, with another, Gwen herself; and it parallels in its growth Annie's increasing hatred of and distance from her mother. The morning of the day she begins to menstruate also marks the entry of the figure of the serpent, a figure which will be repeated later in the text, with continued reference to the mother. The schoolgirl habit of taking recess among the tombstones glosses further the association of Annie with death and separation, for here she is metonymically sitting among the dead, a figure reinforced by the "tolling" of the school bell, and the return to class "as if going to a funeral." The concluding words of Chapter Three, that "I could not understand how she could be so beautiful even though I no longer loved her" underscore this process of separation and detachment, valorizing dream and reality, and taking the narrative, both literally and figuratively, to a point of no return.

Annie's paradoxical love for the Red Girl embodies her new-found delight in evil and rebellion, for she befriends her precisely because her appearance and personal hygiene belie everything that Annie's mother had ever taught her: "her dress was dirty . . . the red hair . . . was matted and tangled . . . her fingernails held at least ten anthills of dirt under them . . . She had such an unbelievable, wonderful smell, as if she had never taken a bath in her whole life." She personifies all the personal and practical negatives which would spur on Annie's revolt against maternal repression, and Annie associates with her to further this end. The reference to the Red Girl playing marbles against Skerritt boys—this being a term referring to boys of the local juvenile reform school, located on Skerritt's estate—associates Annie, in effect, through a double metonymy mediated by the Red Girl, with the principles and practices of evil and criminality, and crowns her efforts at self-identity to this point. For Annie's activities are directed toward nothing else but the achievement and attainment of a valid self-identity and self-image. Her energies, as they are represented here, are signs of actions aimed at the accomplishment of this goal. Once again we see the return of the repressed, wish-fulfillment translated into both deed and word: Gwen remained her friend "in spite of" her mother's approval, and because of her "shyness," which went along with Annie's practice of "betrayals," through which reference she tropes and repeats her perception of her mother's actions. But signs of repression manifested through word and deed also take different forms; the sadomasochistic activities practiced by Annie with the Red Girl may be interpreted as a dual sign pointing to an attempt at individualism and self-assertion, as well as the purchase of pleasure, two things which the metamorphosis in the maternal relationships were denying her.

Here, the continued repression of her unconscious desire manifests itself in actions of a more overt nature. Later, when her habit of playing marbles is discovered by her mother, she speaks of her parents talking about her "as if I (weren't) there sitting in front of them, as if I had boarded a boat for South America without so much as a goodbye," a phrase which is a tropological representation of the actions of Annie's father's parents. A little later, she also makes a passing reference to the fate of her mother's brother, who had died some time before. What we see here, in the repetition and refiguration to her late uncle, is a resurfacing of the original manifestation of Annie's desire for separation and identity, as evidenced through the death images which have surrounded and beset her at previous points in the narrative. In other words, repression is a permanent and component part both of Annie's thinking and of her narrative, which recounts that thinking. Her methodical revelations of the process which, incorporating this repression, would lead to her attainment of a valid functioning identity, and her use of the tropes and figures attached to this process, thus mediate both her past and her future in narrative terms.

The test of wills that the episode of the marbles, with its embedded serpent narrative, touches off, signifies first the attainment of a certain equality on the part of the two combatants; a sort of halfway point in the battle for supremacy is suggested by the exchange of equally warm, treacherous voices. The embedded narrative of the snake, however, signifies a psychological gambit on the mother's part, one that comes very close to being successful. By establishing a valorized self, and then proceeding to place a threat in close proximity to it, the mother succeeds in playing on the remnants of Annie's repressed love for her, causing Annie to set up a parallel between the snake and her own lies and deception, to feel guilt at this wonderful creature of whom she was taking advantage, and to be tempted to admit to her mother's accusations. Through the repetition of embedding as thematic juxtaposition, the mother's narrative comes tantalizingly close to achieving its objective by playing on a perception of repressed desire. This may be contrasted with the embedding of the dream sequence which appears slightly later in the narrative. Here, the fact of the dream as dream is taken into account in the narrative: "I had been taught by my mother to take my dreams seriously. My dreams were not unreal representations of something real; my dreams were a part of, and the same as, my real life." The repressed wish, stemming from the revelations inherent in the feminine oedipus and voiced in the words, "My mother would kill me if she got the chance. I would kill my mother if I had the courage," confronts the remnants of love and security which that original maternal smothering signified, and this leads to the rejection of the impulse inherent in "I would say the same words, but slower and slower and in a sad way." Here, incipient action is deflected by what may be termed enduring positive memories.

Nor should we overlook the "Columbus in Chains" episode. Annie recounts her classroom prank in which she disfigured a textbook drawing of Christopher Columbus, with the addition of a caption representing her mother's description of the mother's father in Dominica, Pa Chess. The caption reads: "The Great Man Can No Longer Just Get Up And Go." This is not only a further instance of the repetition-compulsion, but also defiance of authority and the setting up of a prohibition on travel through which Annie will break on the occasion of her own departure. By taking on established authority from one culture and imposing her own (written) will upon it, Annie in effect prefigures her eventual treatment of her mother's authority—by force of will, she rewrites the maternal paradigm, the clash of cultures signifying a portent of the mean by which she engages in validating her own identity.

These conflicting and repressed desires may be compared, in their turn, to Annie's dream when the Red Girl departs. This sequence repeats elements of her mother's boat trip from Dominica to Antigua, as well as certain key aspects of Annie's own dream of separation from her mother. Such compulsive repetitions are signs of a desire for difference and for an independent identity, which will be fulfilled ineluctably through repetition of past events in her own particular context. Dream, embedded narrative, and main text thus intertwine to generate this myriad of signs, creating the narrative paradox that is both Annie John and *Annie John*.

The revelation that Annie, in her childhood, had been closely and physically associated with the narrow escape from death of a close friend, involving a reproduction of a criminal hanging, allows a clearer evaluation both of the reasons for and the results of her repression of the incident. It also elucidates the morbid imagery in which this repression would be couched when it periodically surfaced. In other words, the preponderance of death images as responses to psychological stimuli very likely has its root cause in this incident. The subsequent argument between Annie and her mother, during which Annie "could see the frightening black thing leave her to meet the frightening black thing that had left me," marks the inception of the final stage of the protracted oedipal battle which has been the main subject of this narrative. The "black things," fragmented, synechdochal representations of the two female rivals, their negative, contentious potential prefigured by the repression-linked death images, are signs of the final split which is taking place, the beginning of identity-formation and-assumption: "The two black things joined together in the middle of the room separated, hers going to her, mine coming back to me." The oedipal process works through the repression images, making self-generation and independence perceptible: "it was as if the ground had opened up between us, making a deep and wide split. On one side of this split stood my mother . . . on the other side stood I."

This split is the final stage of the oedipal conflict and the desire for an individual identity which the narrative has traced subsequent to the primal scene. Annie's awareness of her mother's "difference" is cemented further just prior to this episode by her mother's calling her "a 'slut' (in patois)" until it engenders a response in kind. Her new-found sense of equality and individuality are the culmination of this protracted oedipal struggle, permitting her to repudiate the maternal envelopment to which she had been subjected and finally to assume a subject position. And this change in status means, also, that she must act. Now her existential awareness of the furniture in her room leads to what is undoubtedly the major psychological event of the novel: her demand that her father make her her own trunk. This demand is the overwhelming, preponderant sign of Annie's desire finally to escape and overcome the containment, possession and control that her mother's trunk signifies. Establishing her own life and identity will constitute a sort of rebirth, phoenix-like, from the deathly images and fears of dissolution which had haunted her for so long.

Chapter Seven charts the progress of this rebirth, the pupal stage which is necessary before the formation of the chrysalis and the emergence of the butterfly. Several striking figures mediate this process. First among these is Annie's vision, in her delirium, of the death of her parents' word: "I could see the words leave their mouths. The words traveled through the air towards me, but just as they reached my ears they would fall to the floor, suddenly dead." Now, if the parental word signifies the Law of the Father, the ultimate sign of authority and power, then Annie has effectively removed herself as subject to this law: not only does the word not reach her, it dies of its own accord. Both parental and paternal authority—the later exercised here by the mother—are laid to rest finally and permanently. The erasure of the photographs on her night-table derives its significance from the areas removed from the bodies. By erasing her mother and father "from the waist down," she takes revenge on the primal scene, immobilizing them and negating their physical and sexual power.

The dyadic fusion betrayed by the mother in that scene now has been abrogated to herself, as she proceeds to separate herself from long-familiar people, places, and objects. The new state of the wedding picture, where "none of the people . . . except for me, had any face left," signifies Annie's final separation from all her relatives, the severing of familiar and familial ties to ensure the survival of her new identity and independence. Finally, the erasure of herself in the confirmation picture "except for the shoes" signifies her renouncing of her old existence and her adoption of the new, the survival of her shoes prefiguring her imminent departure. The process of rebirth reaches its conclusion at the rain's end, where all is regenerated, fresh and

new—including herself, for she has grown, physically as well as psychologically. She now has succeeded in repudiating every aspect of her former life;
both Antigua, the locus of repression, and her mother, the cause of it, must
be rejected in order that this newly-created self might flourish in fresh
surroundings. Remaining would have nullified any attempt at renewal. Every
element of that existence is linked to the stifled, enclosed nonentity she had
been before: "I was feeling . . . how much I never wanted to see my mother
. . . how much I never wanted to hear her voice again." With rebirth, repression has disappeared and desire, formerly sublimated, is untrammelled and
now, marked by a new wish to be other, for the security of complete
anonymity: "I longed to be in a place where nobody knew a thing about me
and liked me for just that reason." Only the freedom of being unknown can
assure the avoidance of past errors.

Annie's complete alienation—even from her close friend, Gwen—on
the day of her departure is the final sign of her rejection of the old and acces-
sion to the new. Even such friendships, formerly valorized as signs of repression and rebellion, now can find no place in the new order. Significantly, her
new trunk, a metonym of her new identity and the existence she is about to
begin, precedes her to the jetty. Her walk there becomes a sort of triumphal
parade, a recounting and dismissal of the life she is leaving behind, as well as
a troping of her mother's departure from Dominica at a similar age years
before. Such repetition is necessary for the wheel to come full circle, for
Annie to establish her own separation from the non-differentiated structure
of which she previously had been a part. There is a final ambiguity in her
double reading of the realization that "I shall never see this again," one which
is extended into the text's final metaphor. The figure of the "vessel filled with
liquid (which) had been placed on its side and now was slowly emptying out"
embodies ambivalence, writing itself as sorrow, relief, release, joy, or any
combination or permutation of the above. Oedipal repression and racial
difference as a subset of "foreignness," the overriding tropological constructs
of the novel, finally allow self-assertion pride of place.

How then can one summarize the resonances of this remarkable text?
The linking of the repression and recognition inherent in the feminine
oedipal paradigm to the problematics of race and culture particular to the
Caribbean region figures in the text in two fundamental ways, it seems to me.
First, the psychological grounding of the text in the feminine oedipus
provides a springboard from which to broach problems of some significance.
The question of the oedipal nature of mother/daughter relationships is one
which figures strongly in women authors of several bicultural contexts, and
is an almost constant signifier of the struggle to establish an identity which
is independent of the mother, and of the clash of cultures. With her mother

fulfilling what was in essence a phallic role, enveloping Annie's budding personality and giving it no chance to flower, turning Annie into a simple extension of herself, Annie had no opportunity for identity, no possibility of establishing a valid, functioning persona. Once the primal scene had brought her situation to the forefront of her consciousness, placing her mother under the rubric of betrayal, difference, and loss of power, her need to establish her own identity was inevitable. Death and separation, repeated tropological representations of the repressed nature of Annie's desire to replace identification with the (m)other and full subjectivity, persistently would figure crucial points on her road to selfhood.

Yet to be contextualized finally is the question of the function of geographical location and cultural setting within the narrative matrix. The heterogeneous structure of Caribbean society and culture, historically linked to the perpetuation of artificial boundaries and divisions among the islands, particularly within a colonial context, would make issues of identity and perceptions of difference dependent each upon the other for their resolution. In this case, the repressive mother was the other in whom the daughter sought images of herself. Given her perceived otherness, "foreignness," and racial difference, and with the primal scene as the locus of this perception, the mother's loss of power and authority would be mirrored by the daughter's concomitant assumption of identity and selfhood. This entire oedipal process is tied inextricably to the cultural matrix, which is itself mediated by perceptions of difference in myriad forms. Indeed, one might observe that the polyvalence which is germane to the Caribbean region is reflected in the structure of the narrative. The West Indian setting, with its own distinct cultural constructs, particularizes both story and discourse as it problematizes its own mode of being.

So it is Kincaid's own Caribbean self-reflective perception which provides the narrative motor for this story for all seasons. The maternal/filial conflict, the attempt to name and to be oneself, the struggle with difference and biculturality, and the repeated use of key tropes, generating the binary oppositions which figure the entire work, all herald a skillful, conscious and controlled narrator, as well as a marvelous addition to the canon of Caribbean literature, which is itself concerned with the crucial questions of naming and being given the polyvalence of its own cultural particularity. Finally, Kincaid herself valorizes the difference of her original cultural and geographical text, which, so to speak, wrote her, so that she could write all of us: "What I really feel about America is that it's given me a place to be myself—but myself as I was formed somewhere else."

EDYTA OCZKOWICZ

Jamaica Kincaid's Lucy: Cultural "Translation" as a Case of Creative Exploration of the Past

In her potent essay "On Seeing England for the First Time," Jamaica Kincaid writes: "The space between the idea of something and its reality is always wide and deep and dark" (37). Her reflection delineates the "space" of complex post-colonial experience which has captured and shaped the lives of many peoples colonized since Christopher Columbus's first conquests. Born on Antigua, a former British colony, Kincaid, as both a writer and an individual, struggles with her legacy of post-colonialism. *A Small Place* (1988) is her insightful critical analysis of political, historical, and cultural aspects of the post-colonial reality on Antigua. Her collection of short stories, *At the Bottom of the River* (1978), and the first novel, *Annie John* (1983), deal with her Antiguan childhood and adolescence. All of them represent an attempt to define the most vital aspects of post-colonial experience: psychological, cultural, and social marginality; political exclusion; racial and sexual discrimination; and the domination by the white man and his culture. *Lucy* (1990) picks up at the point where all her previous works ended and explores the possibilities of transcending the heroine's post-colonial predicament.

Upon immigrating to the United States, a young West Indian woman begins her painful and lonely search for identity. Her struggle for personal freedom and independence entails total, self-imposed separation from her family, particularly her mother, and a commitment to complete detachment.

From *MELUS*, Fall 1996. © 1996 by MELUS.

Such rejection of her former identity and alienation from the past and much of her present experience grant Lucy the independence and freedom to assert herself in a position of control and power, which, in turn, allows her to re-invent her self and create a new future. But her re-invention would not be possible out of a void of self-destruction and loneliness. Though abandonment of her former self is the necessary condition for Lucy's liberation, the conse-quent exploitation and appropriation of her past and present are the vital formative determinants in the process of inventing her new self. They require a form of mental re-colonization of her past and present as a means of repos-sessing them on her own grounds. The binary divisions of center-margin, self-other, good-evil, white-black—the so-called "Manichean aesthetic" that Fredric Jameson sees as characteristic of post-colonial societies and their liter-atures—are particularly evident in Lucy's perceptions of her American present. By the way these binaries traditionally define Lucy's ethnicity/race, gender, and occupation/class, they also inscribe her into the American society as the marginalized "other" before she even reaches the country.

The new dichotomies, however, of memory and intuition, anger and love, despair and freedom construct the boundaries of Lucy's creative exploitation and colonization of her Antiguan past and American present. Her self derives a creative impetus/inspiration from the tension between the abrogation of her memory and its intuitive appropriation, acceptance of her anger and temporary denial of love, and the paradox of freedom found in escape from her despair.

The novel captures Lucy at the cross-roads of cultures and identities (Antiguan and American), at the transitional moment of cultural and psychological "translation"—the concept explored in Eva Hoffman's recent autobiography, *Lost in Translation: A Life in a New Language* (1989). Lucy's role as a translator can be compared to that of the interpreter and post-colo-nial writer, both "caught in the conflict between destruction and creativity" (Ashcroft *et al.* 80), "situated at the ambivalent site of interpretation itself" (83). Consequently, recognized as both a creative and destructive process, "translation" exists only in the form of tension between the forces of abro-gation and appropriation of the old and new simultaneously. And I suggest that in *Lucy* the heuristic significance of the "translation" metaphor is shifted to the unique processes of appropriation as the actual locus of inventing her self.

I look at Kincaid's novel as a form of retracing Lucy's identity to its post-colonial beginnings and opening for her the possibilities of creating a new self through actual exploitation of her post-colonial experience. Although the heroine is not always fully conscious of what is happening to her, the novel clearly defines the whole process of change that her person undergoes, and each of the chapters deals with the consecutive stages of her "translation." The first two chapters ("Poor Visitor" and "Mariah") illustrate Lucy's abrogation of her past, and they re-establish the tension inherent in the colonial dichotomy of colonizer-colonized. These two worlds are still functioning for Lucy in America. They allow the heroine to demystify her disabling position as the colonized and thus initiate her liberation from it.

The middle two chapters ("The Tongue" and "Cold Heart") relate how Lucy invents her own past through further denial of her Antiguan past and an attempt to appropriate it into her American present. Consequently, Lucy gains personal independence, thanks to which, in the last chapter ("Lucy"), she recovers her original sense of identity hidden in "Lucy, a girl's name for Lucifer" (153). Her self-realization triggers the acceptance of her post-colonial past as an important part of who she is and who she may want to become. Coming to America, also a former colony, Lucy can negotiate the multiple influences and possibilities that both destroy and create the reality of her personal identity. She has an opportunity to create a personal space in which she can choose how to exist.

In her review of *Lucy* in the *Village Voice Literary Supplement*, Jane Mendelsohn calls Kincaid's novel "a book about salvation" (21). Although I find Mendelsohn's insights about salvation, purgatory, and guilt important and valid in the context of the book, 1 would like to suggest that *Lucy*, instead of salvation, explores the "space" between the very idea of salvation, shaped by her post-colonial education (for example, reading and memorizing Milton), and its actual reality—the "space" in which one of the predominant experiences is disappointment and the means of surviving it and dealing with it—instead of the experience of relief I would associate with salvation. One of Lucy's first reflections on the January night of her arrival to America illustrates how clear the distinction is for her between the ideas and their reality:

> In a *daydream* I used to have, all these places [that she passes on her way from the airport] were points of happiness to me; all these places were lifeboats to my small drowning soul. . . . *Now that I saw these places*, they looked ordinary, dirty, worn down by so many people entering and leaving them in real *life*. . . . It was not my first bout with the *disappointment of reality* and it would not be my last. (3–4; emphasis added)

Lucy's ability to distinguish between the idea and its reality is necessary to her personal liberation and consequent self-invention. It enables her to recognize who she was told and made to be, who she actually is, and who she wants or does not want to become. From the beginning of Lucy's experience, the focus is directed towards her most extensive inner change as opposed to the external one (her immigration to America).

In America everything is wrong. The sun shines but the air is cold. The songs about love are insincere and artificial, their melodies shallow and words meaningless. Marital relations between Lewis and Mariah, Lucy's employers, appear phony. Despite the fact that everything new Lucy experiences seems to her "such a good *idea* that [she] could *imagine* [she] would grow used to it and like it very much" (4), she feels unhappy, "cold inside and out" (6). Her communication with Lewis and Mariah is incomplete. She perceives and relates to the world through her dreams. Lewis and Mariah replace the actual dream experience of the fantastic and subliminal with Dr. Freud's theories of dream interpretation. Including Lucy, everybody realizes that she is not yet a part of this American reality. They call her the visitor "just passing through, just saying one long Hallo!" (13). At the moment, she feels not only alone and displaced, but she relives the psychological condition of the first settlers in Australia, "a prison for bad people, people so bad that they couldn't be put in a prison in their own country" (9). Her dream about a nightgown "Made in Australia" expresses her deep sense of being degraded below what is considered bad for both the colonizers and the colonized who were successfully brainwashed. She is a mental outcast and moral convict who refuses to accept what she is told to be. For now, she does not "want to take in anything else" (4), and she knows she cannot go back to where she came from.

The following chapter, "Mariah," is haunted by Lucy's post-colonial experience and memory. Including the dream closing the preceding chapter, there are three dreams in the book, in which Lucy is being chased respectively by Lewis, daffodils, and thousands of people on horseback carrying cutlasses to cut her up into small pieces; all three images metaphorically express the aggression of the colonizers and their dominating culture. Lewis represents the white patriarchal culture of the colonizers; daffodils come from Wordsworth's poem Lucy was forced to memorize at school and whose beauty she was told to assimilate without ever seeing the flowers themselves; and the horsemen threaten Lucy with violent dissolution, fragmentation of her person into meaningless pieces—the metaphor for the act of colonization as seen by the colonized. Lucy's perceptions of present reality and her reflections are filtered through her post-colonial perspective. Even though she has left Antigua and denied her mother, post-colonial experience and knowledge are a large part of who she is. Denial and self-dispossession of her past will not liberate her unless she appropriates her past in the process of exploring the present. The first step is her realization and acceptance of the great anger she feels toward her past, which she discovers recalling her childhood experience with daffodils. In the process she is also taught about the inescapability of her post-colonial vision. She cannot but cast the daffodils in "a scene of conquered and conquests; a scene of brutes masquerading as angels and angels portrayed as brutes . . . [and] nothing [can] change the fact that where [Mariah sees] beautiful flowers [Lucy sees] sorrow and bitterness" (30).

The second step toward appropriation of her past requires distancing herself from the past by actively using it in order to avoid being taken in by her present. The awareness of her past allows her to see simultaneously both the idea and the reality of the present she is living. For example, on their way to the Great Lake, when Lucy, Mariah and the children eat dinner in the dining car, Lucy notices how the diners all look "like Mariah's relatives" (32), and the people waiting on them look like hers. Yet on closer observation, she realizes that "they are not at all like her relatives; they only *look* like them" (emphasis added). Lucy notices that Mariah does not and cannot share her perspective, because she is inscribed by the dominant colonizer's world and accepts the conqueror's status:

> She acted in her usual way, which was that the world was round
> and we all agreed on that, when I knew that the world was flat
> and if I went to the edge I would fall off. (32)

Although there is no sense of danger in Mariah's world, Lucy's is not only a backward, flat world, but dangerous to her. Her observation again confirms the strong sense of two unbreachable worlds and the inescapable post-colonial dichotomy of colonizer-colonized, which Lucy has to transcend in her struggle for the freedom of self-invention.

Lucy's relationship with Mariah is a complex reflection of the above processes further complicated by her struggle to cut herself off from her mother and everything she could love,

> for I didn't want to love one more thing in my life, I didn't want
> one more thing that could make my heart break into a million
> little pieces at my feet. (23)

Deep in her heart, Lucy loves her mother. On occasions she acts like her mother (feeding one of the girls) and almost becomes her. Nevertheless, her mother belongs to her past, and Lucy harbors a lot of anger towards her, anger which, until it is explained and understood by her, makes her translate her love for her mother into hatred and then an actual physical and mental separation.

Mariah serves as a surrogate mother for Lucy in this transitional moment of her liberation and self-invention. She makes up for the short-comings of Lucy's real mother. For example, Lucy can express and discuss her sexuality with Mariah without being repressed by the overpowering sense of moral propriety/authority (their conversation over the vase of flowers or Lucy telling Mariah about her sex life with Paul). Mariah also respects Lucy's independence. She does not restrict her freedom to choose friends even if Mariah herself does not like them (Lucy's friendship with Peggy). Consequently, Lucy loves Mariah for being for her what her real mother could not be. At the same time, however, when Mariah tries to teach Lucy to see things through her eyes, Lucy recognizes that

> I already had a mother who loved me, and I had come to see her love as a burden and had come to view with horror the sense of self-satisfaction it gave my mother to hear other people comment on her great love for me. I had come to see that my mother's love for me was designed solely to make me into an echo of her; and I didn't know why, but I felt that I would rather be dead than become just an echo of someone. (36)

Lucy's independence from Mariah is further assured by her clear sense of their being inscribed by the colonial dichotomy. It is inescapable on the outside; Lucy's blackness sharply contrasts with her angelic vision of Mariah:

> Mariah, with her pale-yellow skin and yellow hair, stood still in this almost celestial light, and she looked blessed, no blemish or mark of any kind on her cheek or anywhere else, as if she had never quarreled with anyone over a man or over anything, would never have to quarrel at all, had never done anything wrong and had never been to jail, had never had to leave anywhere for any reason other than a feeling that had come over her. (27)

Lucy's description of Mariah is emblematic of the way she relates to her. Her initial judgments are superficial and totally controlled by colonial brainwashing; the impulse to speculate ("as if") initiates independent thinking through the basic method of comparison and contrast between what she is told to see and what she actually sees. The power of her personal experience liberates Lucy from the illusion created by the post-colonial idea of Mariah. She enters her reality by switching the dichotomy of Mariah—strong—smelling good and Lucy—weak—smelling "bad," when she concludes:

The smell of Mariah was pleasant. Just that—pleasant. And I thought, But that's the trouble with Mariah—she smells pleasant. By then I already knew that I wanted to have a powerful odor and would not care if it gave offense. (27)

Lucy does not look at Mariah as a figure of maternal authority, as she had to see her real mother. She investigates not who Mariah or her authority are, but how she got to be the way she is: made to feel alive by flowers bending in the breeze; made miserable because the weather does not live up to her expectations; beyond any doubt or confidence; "the sort of victor who can claim to be the vanquished also" (41). Lucy's questions are another form of establishing and securing her independence from Mariah, even when her authority is not fully expressed as the white colonizers'. The sense of independence from Mariah is Lucy's small triumph, very important in her struggle for personal independence at the moment, although hollow later, when she recognizes that Mariah is also the victim of one of the many variations of colonial dichotomy, that of man-woman (141–43).

The first two chapters serve as Lucy's orientation in time and her personal space. She distances herself from her past not only by "putting enough miles between them, but also by putting enough events" (31); I interpret "them" as "mental events," Lucy's moments of clear distinction between the world she comes from and the one in which Mariah lives, her recognition of the "space" between the idea and its reality. Further, through abrogation of her past and its appropriation into her perceptions of the present, Lucy defines them both as "something heavy and hard . . . [which she comes to think is] the beginning of living, real living" (24–25); as opposed to living someone else's idea of reality or their reality itself. In consequence, Lucy gains certain independence from both her past and present since she lives them both at the same time. Her important and permanent triumph is the realization about the meaning of her American experience: "It was my past, so to speak, my first real past—a past that was my own and over which I had the final word" (23).

The following chapter "Tongue" deals with the complexities of change Lucy undergoes. Once she covers the "space" between the idea of unchangeability and its reality—"Everything remains the same and yet nothing is the same" (78)—she feels that her present change might be as inevitable and out of her control as her adolescent experiences of physical maturation (e.g., first pubic and under arm hair, first menstruation). Yet, she puts herself in charge of her change by making, from the start, a vital distinction: "Taste is not the thing to seek out in a tongue; *how it makes you feel*—that is the thing" (44; emphasis added). Instead of shaping her judgments solely by the general nature of her experiences, she focuses on the feelings they produce in her and thus provides herself with the immediate means to personal liberation. For example, she loves Miriam from the very first moment they meet. Even though Lucy's only explanation is that Miriam "must have reminded [her of herself when she] was that age" (53), her free and unconditional love for the girl reflects and activates her need and capacity for self-love, the first condition of becoming one's own person. She also defines and accepts her love for Mariah: "Mariah reminded me more and more of the parts of my mother that I loved" (59). Consequently, she recognizes that she feels both love and hatred for her own mother. In order to deal with these conflicting feelings, she knows that she has to maintain her total separation from the family at any cost. For example, she does not answer nor even open her mother's letters. However, besides dealing with the complexities of her relationship with the mother, her growing to love Mariah also means that Lucy can look beyond Mariah as a representative of the colonizers. She admits that even though "it could be said that [Mariah's] kindness was the result of her comfortable circumstances, many people in her position [would not be] as kind and considerate as she was" (72–73). Lucy has to transcend the colonial dichotomy in order to appreciate Mariah as an individual.

Lucy is very careful when dealing with love, particularly one that could limit her personal freedom:

> I could tell that being in love would complicate my life just now.
> I was only half a year free of some almost unbreakable bonds, and
> it was not in my heart to make new ones. (71)

She avoids falling in love with Hugh for the same reason that she refused to give up her virginity to Tanner; she "could not give [them] such a hold over [her]" (83). She struggles to liberate herself from the influence of her own feelings towards others. Such self-denial, commitment to detachment and not missing anyone or anything grant Lucy her total personal independence, flexibility, and freedom to choose how to create herself.

Consequently, Lucy develops her friendship with Peggy despite Mariah's disapproval; she starts smoking cigarettes and explores her sexuality. For the first time since she had left home, she feels happy (51). Her initial attraction to the insincere and artificial (11) is transformed into an acute awareness of the dishonest, hollow, and phony. She easily perceives the general "untruths" in the family life of Lewis and Mariah (47, 77). Again, she is in a position to recognize the "space" between the idea and its reality with exquisite sharpness. It is clear to Lucy that Lewis and Mariah's love is unreal, the ideal they often perform for each other as a show, especially when Lewis and Dinah (Mariah's best friend) betray Mariah, a painful reality Mariah sees too late.

Lucy would not be able to have such insights into Mariah's, Lewis's and Dinah's characters without the wisdom she brought from Antigua. Yet only with her newly gained emotional freedom can she appropriate that wisdom from her past in a way that furthers her ability to distinguish between the idea and its reality in her present, the untruth and truth which she has to sort out before she can create her new and independent self.

"Cold Heart" is a form of final good-bye to Lucy's Antiguan past. She realizes that "just a change in venue" (90) is not sufficient to liberate her. She has to create, not only separate and change herself. Like Kincaid herself, Lucy does not "make up a past that [she does not] have. [She] just [makes her] present different from [her] past" (Bonetti Interview 133). First, she rejects not only being like her mother but her mother herself, since she personifies her past. Out of both present happiness and disillusionment, she proclaims herself "alone in the world and I shall always be this way—all alone in the world" (93). After the death of her father, Lucy's state of total loneliness means self-imposed motherlessness and real fatherlessness; again the idea opposes reality.

When creating her present as different from her own past, Lucy allows herself to feel and act opposite to what her mother had taught her. Upon meeting Paul, her future lover, she says

> "How are you?" in a small, proper voice of the girl my mother had hoped I would be: clean, virginal, beyond reproach. But I felt the opposite of that, for when he held my hand and kissed me on the cheek, I felt instantly deliciously strange; I wanted to be naked in a bed with him. (97)

Later on she betrays Paul with Roland, a salesman from the camera shop, and lives the life her mother warned against: becoming a slut. She also chooses Paul over Peggy, despite her mother's teachings: you "should never take a man's side over a woman's" (48). She freely talks to Mariah, who is now like "a good mother" to her (110), about her sexual life with Paul. In the process of all these actions, Lucy liberates herself from the implications and moral judgements inscribed into her relationships when defined by binary oppositions of mother/daughter, man/woman, male love/female friendship.

The appearance of Maude Quick, her mother's ideal goddaughter and Lucy's "personal jailer" in her childhood (111–12), brings Lucy to her ultimate rejection of her mother. The tragic news of her father's death only momentarily undermines her self-confidence. Maude's remark that Lucy reminds her of Miss Annie triggers all the hatred, hostility, and anger towards her mother that was building up in her. She bursts:

> "I am not like my mother. She and I are not alike. She should not
> have married my father. She should not have had children. She
> should not have thrown away her intelligence. She should not
> have paid so little attention to mine. She should have ignored
> someone like you [Maude Quick]. I am not like her at all." (123)

As the father has left her mother a pauper, Lucy sends her all her money and a letter enumerating all the ways in which she thinks her mother betrayed herself and her daughter as well. To Lucy, her mother's betrayal of her only daughter, someone of her own kind, another woman, is not only unforgivable but irreparable. Lucy's separation from Mrs. Judas, the name she gives her mother, is necessary and inevitable, even though probably never complete.

The chapter ends with a kind of epiphany, Lucy's tragic yet liberating self-realization that her

> life was at once something more simple and more complicated
> than [the dictionary definition of a "woman" given her by
> Mariah]: for ten of her twenty years, half of [her] life, [she] had
> been mourning the end of a love affair, perhaps the only true love
> in [her] whole life [she] would ever know. (132)

It is hard to judge if Lucy means a love affair with her mother or with being a woman, or perhaps being in love with herself and her mother as women. Here again, like Kincaid herself when she talks about her fiction, Lucy aims "to be true to something . . . [when she is] trying to understand how [she] got to be the person [she is]" (Bonetti Interview 125–26). Both the writer and her heroine perform a kind of creative act when they search for and invent certain truths about themselves.

In her struggle to maintain her personal independence, Lucy identifies herself against some artistic models. With Gauguin, she shares the yearnings of "wanting something completely different from what you are familiar with, knowing it represents a haven" (95). However, she quickly rejects "the perfume of the hero about" Gauguin and recognizes that he is an inadequate model for someone like herself, "a young woman from the fringes of the third world, who left home wrapped in the mantle of a servant." She also does not identify herself with the artists she meets at Paul's, "very chatty people who talk about themselves and the world and take it for granted that everything they say matters" (98); they are also mostly men. She knows that she is not and does not want to be this kind of an artist; but she "shall always like to be with the people who stand apart." Her recollection of the Myrna story further shows Lucy's early fascination with the unique (in her child-hood meaning the forbidden and secret experiences). Her search to be different, to have something of her own, testifies to her desperate need to create her existence separate from her mother's.

Finally, Lucy's interest in photography liberates her imagination to see the extraordinary in the pictures of "ordinary people in a countryside doing ordinary things" (115). Now on the creative, artistic plane, Lucy is compelled to ask the same old question about the "space" between the idea and its reality: "Why is a picture of something real eventually more exciting than the thing itself?" (121). This time, however, she wonders about the direction, orientation of the "space" in question, a kind of creative order that gives the "space" its meaning.

It is interesting to notice how Lucy's search for personal freedom is first generalized as a "part of the whole human situation" (129), only to be ironi-cally telescoped by her memory's ever-present lens of colonial experience. Lucy seems to believe that all kinds of freedom are arbitrary and individual. For example, she wants to warn Mariah not to count on that "free" feeling she has after her divorce from Lewis, because it can vanish like a magic trick. She is also surprised to hear Paul saying that the great explorers/colonizers conquered the world not only in search of riches but also to feel free. In her mind, the originally noble urge to freedom often leads people away from it; paradoxically, sometimes freedom can only be found in death. The image of dead wild animals on both sides of the highway metaphorically expresses her tragic vision of human striving for freedom. But Lucy's personal example shows that the individual's struggle for freedom is the only means to mean-ingful and creative existence. Thus, the tentative orientation of Lucy's "space" points towards the universally human contained within the highly personal and individual experience; it rejects the linear in favor of recursive and spiral order/construction of the "space" between the idea and its reality.

The closing chapter of the novel again presents Lucy "making a new beginning" (133), exactly a year after her arrival in America. There are signif-icant external changes: Lucy moves to a new apartment with Peggy and gets a job as a secretary; she becomes socially and economically independent. Yet, much more important changes take place inside of her mind and memory. Although she does not know the person she has become very well, for the first time she entertains the idea that she might be beautiful. She also rede-fines her relationship with her past, both the Antiguan and last year's Amer-ican one. According to Lucy, the past is "a collection of people you used to be and things you used to do" (137), and therefore she concludes that "your past is the person you no longer are, the situations you are no longer in." Such definition of the past allows her the distance necessary to understand and re-evaluate her colonial history and post-colonial education, so she can appropriate them into her new identity. In the span of less than two pages, Lucy communicates her self-realizations:

> I had come to believe that people in my position in the world should know everything about the place they are from. (134–35)

> I had realized that the origin of my presence on the island—my ancestral history—was the result of a foul deed; but that was not what made me . . . I was not a Briton and that until not too long ago I would have been a slave. (135)

> I understand the situation better now, I understand that, in spite of those words [liberty, equality, and fraternity], my pen pal [from the neighboring French island] and I were in the same boat. (136)

She also draws a line separating the past from present in respect to the last year spent in the household of Lewis and Mariah, she refers to this time of her life repeatedly using the phrase "I used to." Consequently, Lucy is no longer separated but liberated from the direct influence of her past. Using Kincaid's own words, Lucy seems to have succeeded in her struggle for personal freedom, the "struggle to make sense of the external from the things that have made you what you are and the things that you have been told are you" (Vorda Interview 9).

The final chapter resonates with far more poignant meanings than just Lucy's repossession of her past. It reveals her further and deeper involvement in self-invention:

> I understood that I was inventing myself, and that I was doing this more in the way of a painter than in the way of a scientist. . . I could only count on intuition. . . . I had memory, I had anger, I had despair. (134)

To identify her new self, she goes back to her original name: Lucy Josephine Potter (her full birthname is finally mentioned on page 149). Lucy's memories and thoughts about her name give insight into the most private regions of her identity. She recalls her unsuccessful attempt at re-naming (150) and revives the one moment from her childhood when she knew who she was:

her mother's angry confession, "I named you after Satan himself. Lucy, short for Lucifer" (152). Although she has never grown to like "Lucy, a girl's name for Lucifer" (153), it was the only part of her name she cared to hold on to. Not because she felt guilty, as Mariah suggests; she "did not feel like a murderer; [but because she] felt like Lucifer, doomed to build wrong upon wrong" (139). It is one of the first and more complicated judgments that Lucy places on herself after she finds out, again from Mariah, that not only can others judge us, but we can judge ourselves, too. Although the figure of Lucifer comes from the culture of her colonizers, Lucy, now liberated, can freely choose to identify herself with him. The male traits of Lucifer that seem to communicate with Lucy's present situation most significantly are his total alienation and loneliness after the rebellion against God, the result of his uncontainable search for knowledge. Similarly, in consequence of her rebellion against her mother, separation from her Antiguan past, and subsequent attitude of complete detachment and independence, Lucy finds herself liberated but totally alone at the end of the novel. Her state of loneliness and alienation is the price she has to pay for her search for self-knowledge. Like Lucifer, she is fully committed to the task of knowing: "If I did not know *everything* yet, I would not be afraid to know everything as it came up" (153).

Consequently, Lucy courageously withstands her disappointments with reality. Using her camera, she still tries to make the picture of reality more beautiful than the reality itself in hope of finding the things she had not seen with her eyes. She takes to drinking coffee all the time and eating cold, mushy lunches, even though she knows they are not good for her. Her present life style is winding down but free. She is alone and not happy but independent; for Lucy, her freedom and independence are "not a small accomplishment. [She] thought [she] would die doing it" (161).

In the end, neither Lucy nor the reader appears fully gratified to see her suffer from loneliness and unhappiness for the sake of her personal freedom, freedom which, so far, has been defined primarily by rejection, separation, and alienation. Resurrecting her birthname also does not seem a substantial foundation for her new self. Significantly, it becomes "one great blur" (164) as she weeps over the first page of the notebook she got from Mariah.

Although the novel covers one complete stage of Lucy's life, the heroine's character is less complete at the end of her story than at its beginning. The closing picture of Lucy writing in her diary suggests that the story of her self-invention has yet to be created and told by Lucy herself. At this point, even her name seems meaningful only in terms of her past. With her one sentence "I wish I could love someone so much that I would die from it," Lucy draws another line separating her past/s from the present and future.

She closes one way of her existence and self-invention to begin a new one.

Given the somewhat inconclusive experience of Lucy, one has to wonder if there is something inevitably incomplete in cultural and psychological "translation" defined primarily by the exploration of one's past. It is also highly questionable if Lucy's exploration of her past/s has indeed created anything, a new self or self-history, unless we perceive one's control over the past as a precondition of self-invention, creating a new personal "space" in which Lucy's selfhood does not have to be defined by the roles of either colonized or colonizer.

DONNA PERRY

Initiation in Jamaica Kincaid's Annie John

Two recent studies attempt to trace the mythic patterns contained in women's fictions, particularly those written by white, middle-class, Western women: Annis Pratt's *Archetypal Patterns in Women's Fiction* (1981) and Rachel Blau DuPlessis's *Writing beyond the Ending* (1985). These studies are significant not because they can help us better understand *Annie John* (or the work of other black women writers) but because they so clearly outline the parameters of the so-called Western tradition in literature. A short summary of the texts will demonstrate what I mean.

Annis Pratt singles out two dominant patterns in novels of development written by women. The first, the "growing down" story, is the conservative extreme, a model of how to prepare for marriage, behave, and learn humility, stoicism, and self-abnegation. The message is that submission to suffering and sadism prepares one for life; an example is Fanny Fern's popular *Rose Clark* (1856). The more common pattern in women's fiction, according to Pratt, is the move from the green (matriarchal) world, which is restorative, positive, and nourishing, to the enclosed patriarchal world. The message here is that the world of nature belongs to women, but no other world does. Nature keeps women in touch with their selfhood, but this state of innocence is usually destroyed with the onslaught of the patriarchal world. Often there is a "green world" lover (who is more desirable than the socially

From *Caribbean Women Writers: Essays from the First International Conference.* © 1990 by Calaloux Publications.

acceptable one), and a rape trauma is necessary to overturn the matrilinear society. Examples would be Emily Bronte's *Wuthering Heights* (1847) and Margaret Atwood's *Surfacing* (1972). These nature myth narratives are rooted in Greek mythology in which the woman, raped by the gods, turns herself into another life form (Daphne becoming a laurel tree after her rape by Apollo, for example). Sometimes the women find solace, companionship, and independence in nature.

DuPlessis explores the way Western women writers subvert the marriage plot of the novel through themes of reparenting, female bonding, mother-child dyads, and brother-sister pairs. She studies a number of modern texts in which women "find themselves" in ways other than through romance (Dorothy Richardson's *Pilgrimage*, the fiction of Virginia Woolf, the poetry of H.D. and Adrienne Rich). But, as she demonstrates, often the cost for these women is great—the female protagonist may remain isolated, commit suicide, or go insane.

The problem with these two studies is that they look, for the most part, at the writing of white middle- and uppermiddle-class women who saw themselves as part of a literary tradition that glorified marriage and romantic love. DuPlessis spends only fourteen pages out of two hundred on Zora Neale Hurston, Gwendolyn Brooks, Toni Morrison, and Alice Walker, and Pratt cites Paule Marshall, Margaret Walker, Hurston, and Morrison only in passing.

I am suggesting that fiction by women of color and Third World women offers new myths of female development and new definitions of success. As Paule Marshall and Alice Walker have demonstrated, black women have been forced outside the "happily ever after" world of white middle-class privilege to find the story of their lives closer to home. Both describe turning to their mothers for those stories. Marshall recalls learning from "the poets in the kitchen," her mother and the other women from Barbados, who urged one another to talk ("Soully-gal, talk yuh talk!") and gained power through their language ("In this man world you got to take yuh mouth and make a gun!"). Walker found her mother's life to be poetry, and the "ambitious" gardens she grew were her daughter's legacy. As Walker generalizes: "And so our mothers and grandmothers have, more often than not anonymously, handed on the creative spark, the seed of the flower they themselves never hoped to see: or like a sealed letter they could not plainly read."

Novels by women of color, particularly women from outside the United States, draw on different traditions and reflect a different set of cultural assumptions from those that writers like Pratt and DuPlessis define as universal. In many cultures (West Indian, with its roots in Africa, for example) images of strong, autonomous women abound; women are often seen as powerful, even awe-inspiring. African tradition featured women as tribal leaders and *obeah* women, trained in witchcraft and knowledgeable about herbal medicine and cures. Older women were revered as storytellers and keepers of the family history. In short, a woman functioned in other ways than solely in her relationship to men.

I am suggesting that in fiction by women of color, particularly that written by women who have lived or live outside of the industrialized West, there are other development patterns for women. The "green world" harmony that Pratt describes can survive, if transformed, but DuPlessis's romance plot will wither away. A close study of Jamaica Kincaid's novel *Annie John* (1985) suggests a possible paradigm for female development that represents an alternative to the victim models we find in most recent fiction (and in life).

Annie John, Kincaid's only novel, began as a series of short stories and sketches in the *New Yorker*. It is an initiation tale about a young girl's movement from childhood to maturity—from life in lush, fertile Antigua to her eventual move to London at seventeen, when the novel ends. In one sense, Annie's life is just beginning as she leaves her island home for "civilized" Europe, but her apprenticeship in Antigua has prepared her adequately for the world she will face beyond it.

Three aspects of West Indian culture contribute to Annie's development and empower her to leave home and create an independent life: the storytelling tradition; the tradition of the obeah woman who reads nature's signs (storm, cuts that won't heal) and who curses and cures using the materials of nature (herbs, dead animals); and matrilinear bonding—the strong blood tie of women through the generations.

The storytelling tradition among people connects the present with the past (thus suggesting timelessness and immortality), establishes a sense of community, and testifies to the power of language not only to record but to transform reality.

At an earlier time, an enslaved people had to depend on this oral tradition to transmit and maintain their cultural heritage. The tradition of storytelling is an integral part of African culture and was continued in the West Indies among Africans brought there by British, French, and Dutch colonizers. Its continuation in the United States among West Indian immigrants is clear from Paule Marshall's *Brown Girl, Brownstones* (1959), in which young Selina Boyce learns her ethnic identity from her mother and the other Barbadian immigrant women as they talk in her Brooklyn kitchen. In "The Making of a Writer: From the Poets in the Kitchen" (1983), Marshall says that she first learned the power of language through hearing stories.

Storytelling plays a central part in *Annie John*. In an interview, Jamaica Kincaid said, "Clearly, the way I became a writer was that my mother wrote my life for me and told it to me." Significantly, Kincaid claimed that she never read twentieth-century writers until she left Antigua at age seventeen. Her models were stories she heard—ritual retellings of her own and her people's pasts.

There is very little in *Annie John* about the influence of "traditional" writers Annie studied in school, probably because they had little meaning for her. She is forced to copy out Books I and II of *Paradise Lost* as punishment for her rebelliousness—an example of the Western tradition being used punitively—and the novel she cites as her favorite, *Jane Eyre*, is about a woman who is a rebel. The tradition—predominantly white, male, middle-upper class—could not speak to her as her mother's stories could.

What are the effects of this African storytelling tradition? First, Annie becomes the hero of her own life, in sharp contrast to the fate of Western heroines, who are usually forced into prescribed roles and scripts as Pratt and DuPlessis suggest. Significantly, it is Annie's mother who is the weaver of the tale. In the often-repeated ritual of going through Annie's baby trunk, Annie Senior goes through the contents, piece by piece, holding up each item and recreating her daughter's past through vivid accounts of its significance. The christening outfit, baby bottles (one shaped like a boat), report cards, first notebook, and certificates of merit from school become both relics and omens—symbols of the girl she was and the woman she would become—through her mother's transformative language. The narrator remembers: "No small part of my life was so unimportant that she hadn't made a note of it, and now she would tell it to me over and over again."

But there is method in the telling. The stories woven were designed to stress Annie's assertiveness, her accomplishments, and her independence: the slipped stitch in the christening dress happened when Annie, still in her mother's womb, kicked. Annie's mother creates the myth of Annie for her so that her past becomes as real to her as her present. Like Greek heroes who chanted the litanies of past glories to prepare themselves for battle and to awe their opponents, Annie's mother sings her daughter's praises and empowers the child.

Another function of storytelling in the novel is to provide an impetus for Annie's emergence as a writer. At twelve, she is asked by her British schoolteacher to write an "autobiographical essay." She tells the story of the time she went swimming with her mother and her mother disappeared from view. She recreates the panic she felt when her mother disappeared and the joy when she reappeared. But Annie changes the ending both to suit her audience and to please herself. In life Annie's mother shrugged off the event's significance; in Annie's imaginative reconstruction, mother embraces daughter lovingly. Annie wins the adoration of her classmates and her teacher—teary-eyed, Miss Nelson adds the story to the class's library of books. And Annie manages, through telling and transforming her story, to begin the imaginative reconstruction process that is autobiographical fiction.

The most significant implication of storytelling, the power of language in the book, is that it gives Annie a potential source of resistance. From childhood, Annie uses her imaginative versatility to make up elaborate lies to tell her mother when she disobeys. But, more important, stories become a way to rewrite the history of an oppressed people. In *Resistance and Caribbean Literature* (1980), Selwyn Cudjoe says, "The purpose of colonial education was to prepare obedient boys and girls to participate in a new capitalist enterprise." He quotes Sylvia Wynter, who adds, "To write at all was and is for the West Indian a revolutionary act."

The revolutionary potential of language is dramatically illustrated in an episode entitled "Columbus in Chains," depicting the navigator's ignominious return to Spain after he offended the representative of King Ferdinand and Queen Isabella. The narrator remembers: "How I loved this picture—to see the usually triumphant Columbus brought so low, seated at the bottom of a great boat just watching things go by" (pp. 77–78)

Having seen this picture in her textbook, Annie connects Columbus with patriarchal tyranny in general when she overhears her mother talking about Annie's grandfather. The old man who once dominated her life has now become infirm, according to Annie Senior's sister, who still lives in Dominica. Reading her sister's letter telling her of her father's ill health, Annie's mother laughs and says, "So the great man can no longer just get up and go."

Echoing her mother's scorn of patriarchal privilege, Annie writes under the Columbus picture: "The Great Man Can No Longer Just Get Up and Go." For this rebellious act she is stripped of power (she is removed as class prefect) and made to ingest a heavy dose of Western culture—Books I and II of *Paradise Lost*, which she is forced to copy.

Although neither Annie the child nor Annie the narrator focuses on the full implications of colonization, the racism that was a part of West Indian life, the confusion and anger it caused are evident. The narrator remembers:

> Sometimes, what with our teachers and our books, it was hard for us to tell on which side we really now belonged—with the masters or the slaves—for it was all history, it was all in the past and everybody behaved differently now; all of us celebrated Queen Victoria's birthday, even though she had been dead a long

time. But we, the descendants of the slaves, knew quite well what
had really happened, and I was sure that if the tables had been
turned we would have acted differently; I was sure that if our
ancestors had gone from Africa to Europe and come upon people
living there, they would have taken a proper interest in the Europeans on first seeing them, and said, "How nice," and then gone
home to tell their friends about it. (p. 76)

The narrator's political consciousness is still in an embryonic state,
however, since this childish perception is neither challenged nor commented
on. Although there are hints of outrage at colonial oppression, the book, for
the most part, emphasizes Annie's personal growth, not the political situation
in the West Indies. Jamaica Kincaid is not a "political" writer in the sense
that the Jamaican writer Michelle Cliff is, although these references to
oppression suggest that in later works she might more fully explore the political implications of colonialism. (See note at end.)

A second source of strength for Annie lies in the obeah tradition. Two
facts about obeah deserve note: the obeah was believed to be in communication with the devil and other spirits, and she was thought to have full power
to exempt one from any evils that might otherwise happen.

Annie's mother consults the obeah woman (as well as her own mother
and a friend) when ominous signs appear—a small scratch on Annie's instep
does not heal, a friendly dog turns and bites her, a prized bowl suddenly
slips and breaks. The obeah woman reads and interprets: one of the many
women from her husband's past is putting a curse on them. The cure would
be a ritualistic bath in water in which the barks and flowers of special trees
had been boiled in oils.

As a child, Annie fantasizes about such supernatural power when she is
in love with her secret friend, the unwashed, barefoot, tree-climbing "Red
Girl." When this friend moves away, Annie dreams of rescuing her after a
shipwreck and escaping with her to an island where they can get their
revenge on the adult world: "At night, we would sit on the sand and watch
ships filled with people on a cruise steam by. We sent confusing signals to the
ships, causing them to crash on some nearby rocks. How we laughed as their
cries of joy turned to sorrow" (p. 71).

Like her mother's stories, the obeah woman's charms have the power to
transform reality: they can undo curses, heal wounds, even destroy enemies.
From this obeah tradition Annie learns the power of working with nature, of
trusting in signs and symbols, of trusting one's instincts.

The matrilinear bond between Annie, her mother, and her grandmother proves to be the most empowering force of all. The two women

present striking generational contrasts: Ma Chess, the grandmother, who lives in Dominica, more skilled in obeah than anyone Annie knows, appears in person only once in the novel, though her influence is felt throughout. When Annie becomes seriously ill at age fifteen, her grandmother mysteriously appears "on a day when the steamer wasn't due" and nurses Annie back to health. As Annie's mother had done before, the grandmother feeds and bathes Annie, literally taking her granddaughter back into the womb: "Ma Chess would come into my bed with me and stay until I was myself—whatever that had come to be by then—again. I would lie on my side, curled up like a little comma, and Ma Chess would lie next to me, curled up like a bigger comma, into which I fit" (pp. 125–26).

This image of Annie as a fetus protected by its mother is an apt description of the "paradise" of the early part of the novel, when Annie and her mother lived in harmony. With the onset of adolescence came inevitable mother-daughter tensions, and Annie struggled to free herself from life in her mother's shadow. It is as though the maternal sheltering is surfacing again—symbolically—through the nurturance of the grandmother. This nurturance does not smother the adolescent girl but serves as a source of strength, for she has already become a separate being. Her mysterious illness at the end of the novel corresponds to the death of her child self—a dependent self that must grow into freedom. But her grandmother's nurturing clearly suggests that she is not to break away from her past, as most male artist-heroes do (we think of James Joyce's Stephen Daedalus or D.H. Lawrence's Paul Morel). Instead, she must grow into her new, freer self, with maternal blessing. Remember, it was Annie's mother, earlier in the novel, who encouraged her daughter to become independent.

Annie's mother remains her strongest role model. The older woman left Dominica at sixteen to escape a domineering father and gave birth to Annie, her only child, at thirty, after marriage to a man thirty-five years her senior who already had grown children older than she was. This is no romance plot, at least not in the conventional sense, but one based on mutual respect and admiration.

Like all mothers in all cultures, she tries to train her daughter in proper sexual conduct, respectful behavior, and appropriate customs and rituals, but Annie's mother knows the importance of independence and is strong enough to force her child out of the nest: when Annie is twelve her mother stops their communal baths, dressing alike, and being inseparable. She wants her daughter to become a woman.

In "The World and Our Mothers," in the *New York Times Book Review*, Vivian Gornick claims that mother-daughter struggles are more complex than those between fathers and sons because they are fraught with more ambivalence. Speaking of the child's struggle, she says: "Our necessity, it seems, is not so much to kill our fathers as it is to separate from our mothers, and it is the daughters who must do the separating."

Gornick's thesis is borne out in the recent pioneering work by Nancy Chodorow and others, but she is mistaken when she claims that "nowhere in literature is there a female equivalent of the protagonist locked in successful struggle, either with the father or with the mother, for the sake of the world beyond childhood" (10). This may be true of the fiction of white women, but several women of color have immortalized "successful struggle(s)" between mothers and daughters in fiction and autobiography: I think of Paule Marshall's *Brown Girl, Brownstones* (1959), Maya Angelou's *I Know Why a Caged Bird Sings* (1970), Maxine Hong Kingston's *The Woman Warrior* (1975), and Toni Morrison's *Beloved* (1987), as well as *Annie John*. But the paradigm here is different: in a racist society in which the world beyond the family denies her autonomy, the female hero of color looks to her mother—and the world of women—to find models of strength and survival. As Mary Helen Washington explains the situation of the black woman writer in America:

> The literature of black women . . . is about black women; it takes the trouble to record the thoughts, words, feelings, and deeds of black women . . . and few, if any, women in the literature of black women succeed in heroic quests without the support of other women or men in their communities. Women talk to other women in this tradition, and their friendships with other women—mothers, sisters, grandmothers, friends, lovers—are vital to their growth and well-being.

Whereas Gornick and others, following the lead of modern psycho-analysis, claim that our greatest source of tension and conflict resides in the family, black women writers (and many writers of color) recognize that these familial tensions cannot be seen apart from the broader reality of racism. Thus, for the woman of color, her mother and the women in her family and/or community provide strength, self-confidence, an individual and communal history, and heavy doses of reality. For whatever the tensions these characters encounter at home are minor annoyances compared to their oppression in a racist culture.

Annie John is not an overtly political novel, but it challenges us to reexamine old models of what autonomy means for women. At the end of the novel, seventeen-year-old Annie leaves for London and a career as a nurse. Some readers might say that her initiation has not yet begun—that Antigua has been a womb, a paradise from which she must escape—but I disagree. Annie John is as developed as her mother was at sixteen when she packed her belongings into a single trunk and left home alone. And like her grandmother, she has magical powers—her language can transform her life into art.

Since this essay was written, Kincaid has expressed her political convictions in a nonfiction study of Antigua past and present: *A Small Place* (New York: Farrar, Straus & Giroux, 1988).

HELEN TIFFIN

Cold Hearts and (Foreign) Tongues: Recitation and the Reclamation of the Female Body in the Works of Erna Brodber and Jamaica Kincaid

Recent West Indian literature by women offers a locus of debate over the retrieval of the body from and within western discursive erasure. This erasure of the female body and its possible reclamation is of course central to contemporary feminist debate, and has its own genealogy within feminist discourse. My interest in this question, however, is in the ways in which colonialism's discursive and institutional apparatuses obliterated and continue to obliterate the colonised (specifically female) body, and the counter-colonial strategies by which this "lost" body might be reclaimed. In their fiction Erna Brodber and Jamaica Kincaid anatomize the body's erasure under a colonialist scriptive drive and explore potentials for the re/cognition of corporeality and sexuality.

In *A Small Place* Jamaica Kincaid envisions the colonised body in the imperial library. Addressing the British colonisers and educators directly in the second person, she writes,

> You loved knowledge, and wherever you went you made sure to build a school, a library (yes, and in both of these places you distorted or erased my history and glorified your own) . . .
> . . . If you saw the old library . . . the beauty of us sitting there like communicants at an altar, taking in, again and again, the fairy

From *CALLALOO* 16:4, Fall 1993. © 1993 by The Johns Hopkins University Press.

tale of how we met you, your right to do the things you did, how beautiful you were, are, and always will be. (36, 42)

In such libraries are to be found the ideal colonial readers, obedient subjects who "take in, again and again" the "fairy tale" of a British origination and empire and commonwealth loyalty, the record written by the victors: conquerors, slaveholders. European "fairytales" of all kinds—history, travel narrative, anthropology and literature, the written "records" of relations between Europe and "its" others—were profoundly interpellative. The texts of Europe were both deliberately (and sometimes adventitiously) deployed in the repression of the local and the concomitant reproduction and valorisation of Anglo-European culture at the colonised site, within and through not just the minds but the very bodies of the colonised. Macaulay's infamous "Minute" had in 1835 formulated a British educational policy designed to produce "a class of persons Indian in blood and colour, but English in taste, in opinions, in morals and in intellect" (Macaulay 729). Though this Minute was directed at Indian civil service "minds" (inconveniently situated in Indian bodies) the interpellative effect of colonialist education throughout the empire was frequently to enforce a separation between mind and body in the colonised subject at the same time as it introduced, at least into some societies, the very conception of that separation.

Instructions as to the posture of pupils at desks, physical education and sport marching formations, folk-dancing instruction, and, more cryptically but no less effectively, formal literary recitation, ensured the repression of the colonised and the reproduction of the English body through colonial subjects. The complex history of black-white sexuality within slave-plantation societies plus, in the nineteenth century, Victorian attitudes to sex, effected the particular repression of the black female body and female sexuality. Thus in the twentieth century, the library, the classroom and sexual relations remain the loci of continuing and complex colonialist erasure and repression.

Erna Brodber's "One Bubby Susan" takes anthropologist/historian Frank Cundall's account of an Arawak rock carving and "fleshes out" a counter-interpretation. In the narrator's tale of the origin of this petroglyph, the body of Arawak Susan is reanimated in Creole, instead of in "authoritative" Euro-historical discourse, and the tone is gossipy, not scholarly. In Brodber's version, Susan's history offers an allegory of the extirpation of the female fleshly body under colonialism—both in terms of military invasion and textual capture—leaving only a vague outline in rock. The outline was left by Susan's body when she was stoned to death by her own people for failing to save them from the tragic consequences of European invasion. Susan had earlier rejected her own culture's insistence on women's roles as exclusively those of child-rearer and home-maker and she had abandoned her group to pursue her own life. Alone in her cave, a retreat from the Arawak ideology of family, the solitary Susan ironically becomes an object of religious veneration. But

> Mr Christopher Columbus come with him red rags and all abody . . . It was syphilis that time that come with the tourist rags. People start dropping dead like this and the bad treatment was something else. Man used as target practice! . . .The whiteman was putting their hands and all where they should not be put and on top of that beating up the Arawak men and running their swords through them. (53)

In an ironic combination of the sacred and the profanely-political, spirit and body, the embattled Arawaks begin to treat Susan's excrement as if it were the (mythical) gold the unscrupulous Europeans seek. Susan is denied any privacy and "decide that she not going to be no God with no privacy" (53); the narrative insists on the importance of the body whatever the rewards of spiritual elevation. Susan plays dead, and in disappointment and frustration her people stone her:

> Even when she drop, them still flinging. Even when she so weak she drop oft of the rock face altogether and long time drop into the sink hole, them still seeing her there and still stoning . . . Is now them practice to see if, like the whiteman was doing with them, they could use her for target practice. (53)

Susan's metonymic function in the story is further attested by her final erasure. Even when she is dead "them try to throw stones round what them think is the outline of her body" (53). Her own people, now deeply interpellated by European representations of female corporeality and sexuality, make her shadowy outline the continuing object of their abuse.

The effects of European constructions of the female body within Caribbean communities are the subject of another short allegorical piece by Brodber entitled "Sleeping's Beauty and Prince Charming." Adapting the European fairytale and rewriting its terms and its language, Brodber investigates the legacy of European invasion/representation. The black female body is allegorised as lost through a European textuality so deeply interpellative that black "prince charmings" cannot conceive of or cope with Afro-Caribbean female bodies—their substance has been relegated to a legendary outline which is unseen, ignored, or still often the object of abuse, a fate similar to that of Arawak Susan.

Imaged as "a sightless Samson" Prince Charming of Brodber's parable first perceives Sleeping as simply a "disembodied voice" (2). European textuality/slavery has rendered the black male unable to see black women who have been disembodied by that same history. References to Spenser, the Bible and the fairy tale of "Sleeping Beauty" emphasize the role of Euro-representation in this destructive disembodiment.

In response to historical/textual erasure, Brodber's parable interrogates these European fairy tales adopting (and adapting) the traditional Jamaican concluding formula: "Rastafari me nuh choose none." Invoking both a specifically Jamaican Rastafarian mode, and the notion of "Anancy stories"—an (oral) tradition of a different kind, attesting to the persistence of an Afro-Caribbean folk history/herstory which frequently (though not exclusively) was preserved and passed on by women—"Sleeping's Beauty and Prince Charming" rewrites the European script in a Caribbean narrative mode. The invocation of Anancy also conjures the pejorative relegation by the English colonisers of such Afro-Jamaican folk tales to the category of lies—dangerous lies outlawed in school curricula (and playground circulation) as disruptive of the middle-class English values such educational institutions sponsored. Thus, while Brodber's story inscribes and thematises the persisting effects in the Caribbean of a white education and reading *practice* (from the Bible and European "fairy tales" to contemporary writing by [interpellated] black male West Indians who are thus locked within that Anglo-Scribal tradition, and whose persisting author/ity provides the starting place for Brodber's narrative), it also suggests the possible retrieval, in time, of that lost female body.

Anglo-European textuality and its authoritative institutionalisation not only captured the Afro-Caribbean body within Euro-representation, but severed body from soul. Brodber's "Sleeping" is "a black Ophelia sleeping for seven years" (1). But while her body is comatose/erased, Sleeping's "soul" wanders in search of her "black knight." Though he can feel her eyes on him, can pick up her "heavy vibrations," Charming cannot see her because there is "nobody" (no/body). By the conclusion of the parable, however, this Samson has regained his sight; he can now see black womanhood, though as yet he cannot fully accept her corporeality, her surprising re-embodiment after centuries of erasure; his conditioned apprehension of black woman as shadowy outlines, present only through European representation:

And he left her to be a woman alone, and that is why black people have to wait another four hundred years before King Alpha and Queen Omega will appear to settle them in their kingdom in the promised land. For Sleeping's beauty is still only half awake, drugged in its woman's pain, and she cannot properly put body and soul together, for that needs the help of Charming. (4)

As both these stories attest, the violence, *physical and textual*, of conquest and colonisation destroys cultures, but its impact, though always devastating, is uneven; there is a gender impact difference at the level of the victims. The violence done to others by colonial discourse is also a gendered technology, and gender matters at these moments of textual violence, where cultural genocide often produces a particular violence against women. Once the "fairy tales" of Europe have been internalised, there is often, as in "One Bubby Susan" and "Sleeping's Beauty and Prince Charming," a continuation of colonialist power through local male agency. An inescapable aspect of that violence involves the erasure and abuse of female bodies and female sexuality.

In both Brodber's *Jane and Louisa Will Soon Come Home, Myal,* and in Kincaid's *Annie John* and *Lucy* there is an exploration of this erasure/abuse and the potential for retrieval of the colonised Caribbean body. All four texts trace the processes of female reembodiment and the retrieval of Caribbean voice and body from its entrapment/erasure within European script and from those Anglo-Victorian middle-class values with which an educated Caribbean middle-class were so deeply imbued.

The internalisation of the European text, a process imaged by Kincaid in *A Small Place* through the obedient colonial reader in the European library "taking in again and again the fairy tale of how we met you, your right to do the things you did," is refigured and disrupted in *Annie John* through images of girls in classrooms letting their attention wander from the Anglo-script to sexuality and the body, to female companions and the local boys. Annie and her friends sit on the tombstones of the white planters as they compare and admire their developing breasts. Annie is punished for re-captioning her text-book illustration of Columbus "The Great Man Can No Longer Just Get Up and Go" (78). This is a sentence she has overheard her mother use about *her* father, and it is one Annie redeploys here to suggest her pleasure not just at the reversal of Columbus' fortunes as he is taken back to Europe in chains, but at his strategic disembodiment, his temporary leglessness. Columbus's "discovery" precipitated the atrocities of the slave trade, the kidnapping and transporting of Africans in chains to the Caribbean, and the abuse and erasure of their bodies. In *Annie John* too, Western medical constructions of the body are challenged by competing curative systems, symbolised by the ordering and reordering of medicines in the cabinet during Annie's illness: the first in accord with the more eclectic philosophies of Annie's mother and Ma Jollie; the second by Annie's father (who is more deeply interpellated by the western construction of the body and with medical science's exclusionist philosophy).

In Brodber's *Jane and Louisa Will Soon Come Home* the Victorian legacy of middle class sexual repression, collusive with a history of racist oppression, results in the denial of female sexuality, and is imaged here as a persistent attempt by blacks themselves to eradicate the "black womb," to "breed out" blackness. The result is profound self-denigration and a paranoid repression of sexuality. The children's ring game of "Jane and Louisa" introduces the possibility of overcoming that suppression, and thus of the "homecoming" of sexuality and the retrieval of women's bodies from a brutal history of racism and slavery. Once again a deeply interpellative education system (here tertiary rather than primary, as in *Annie John*) is figured as the institutional agent of a scribal Eurocolonialism that perpetuates the denigration and/or erasure of women's bodies. Alienated from their own bodies, women become speaking puppets of a deeply classed and gendered Anglo-imperialism. And once again it is a return to folkways and to oral Jamaican tradition which counteracts four centuries of damage.

If oral retrieval from scribal oppression and revalorisation of the local from an interpellative foreign education provide the twin modes of restitution, one Anglo-educational strategy in particular deserves attention. In both Brodber's *Myal* and Kincaid's *Lucy*, female school children recite English poetry to approving audiences, and in both novels it is recitation—the learning *by heart* of poetry and its reproduction before audiences—which is depicted as both a technology of interpellation *and* metonymic of the Anglo-colonialist erasure of the black Caribbean female body. It is to the relationship between recitation and oral folk traditions in the Caribbean and their relation to bodily erasure and reincorporation that I now wish to turn.

The reciting of poetry, dramatic set-pieces or prose passages from the works of English writers was not just a practice of literary teaching throughout the empire—one that persisted in "independent" nations into the second half of this century—it was also an effective mode of moral, spiritual and political inculcation. The English "tongue" (and thus English literary culture) was learned "by heart," a phrase that is particularly significant. Through recitation (and catechised questions appended to reading-book material) the colonised absorbed into their bodies ("*hearts*") the "tongue" of the coloniser. Texts, as a number of cultures recognize, actually enter the body, and imperial education systems of this century interpellated a colonialist subjectivity not just through syllabus content or the establishment of libraries within which passive colonials might absorb the lessons of the master, but through memorizing the English script, i.e. taking it into the body and re-producing before audiences of fellow colonials that which had been absorbed by heart/mind. Recitation is thus a ritual act of obedience, usually by a child performer, who in reciting an English litany speaks as if he/she were the imperial speaker/master rather than the subjectified colonial so often represented in those very passages.

In *Myal* Ella O'Grady recites before an approving class and school inspector Kipling's

> Take up the Whiteman's burden
> Send forth the best ye breed
> Go bind your sons to exile
> To serve your captive's need
> To wait in heavy harness
> On filtered folk and wild
> Your new caught sullen peoples
> Half devil and half child (6)

as if she were of the "best breed" and not the "half devil, half child" of imperialist stereotype: "The words were the words of Kipling, but the voice was that of Ella O'Grady aged 13" (5). Such a technology of bodily absorption and cultural reproduction casts colonials not just as obedient *readers* of an English script, but as the obedient re-producers and promulgators of it. And just as school syllabuses, New Critical methodologies of textual analysis, the Cambridge School Certificate and the earlier Civil Service Exams policed the kinds of interpretations of literary texts which were possible in the colonies, so school and public eisteddfod recitations ritualised the *disembodiment* of colonial reading and listening. The "local" body was erased not just by script and performance, but by the necessary assumption on the part of both audience and performer that speakers and listeners were themselves "English." Recitation performance is thus itself metonymic of the wider processes of colonialist interpellation, in the reproduction, at the colonial site of the locally embodied yet paradoxically disembodied imperial "voice," in a classic act of obedience.

The disciplining of the colonised body which accompanied this re-production is also significant. Both boys and girls were expected to recite poetry in school. But the practice of elocution (usually though not always an extracurricular activity), designed to eradicate "ugly" colonial accents, was directed mainly at the production of (middle-class) female speakers whose accents (and sensibilities) would be acceptably upper-class "English." This recitation of poetry both in school and in elocution classes involved a disciplining of the body. Stance, gestures and expressions which mimicked English body movements (albeit exaggerated) were an essential part of the performance.

But at the same time that such rituals of imperial obedience were being sponsored by both English and local education systems which continued British traditions, their ironic doubling yet reversal was being enacted in Caribbean communities through Afro-Caribbean oral performance and Indo-Caribbean dramatic and poetic traditions. These practices, for example the telling of Anancy stories, or indeed, speaking in Creole at all were actively discouraged by schools. Carnival (and Anancy tale-telling) have histories of official and unofficial institutional banning, for while one kind of oral performance—recitation—was an act of obedience, Afro-Caribbean (and to a lesser extent Indo-Caribbean) oral folk performances were regarded as deeply subversive of those imperial ideologies recitation reinforced. Speaking in Creole, even the mention of Anancy (with his "low" associations and subversive potential), was punished in school as an act of *disobedience*, while the reciters of English poetry were applauded.

The interpellation of Ella O'Grady is signalled early in *Myal* by an episode of recitation. Lucy, of Jamaica Kincaid's novel, is also congratulated for her performance of Wordsworth's (post-colonially notorious) "I wandered lonely as a cloud." After Lucy recites the poem to "an auditorium full of parents, teacher, and . . . fellow pupils,"

> everybody stood up and applauded with an enthusiasm that surprised me, and later they told me how nicely I had pronounced every word, how I had placed just the right amount of special emphasis in places where that was needed, and how proud the poet, now long dead, would have been to hear his words ringing out of my mouth. (18)

Recitation not only disciplines the bodies of performers; it also disciplines those of the audience whose appropriate (English) response is invoked by the recitation ritual which combined a peculiar blend of exaggerated peripheral gestures with a formal stance and an Anglo-Victorian appearance of modesty.

By contrast, Afro-Caribbean traditions of dance, tale-telling, carnival did not seek disembodiment, either in terms of manner or matter—rather, the local body could be invoked against the disembodiment of imperialist capture-by-script. Afro- and Indo-Caribbean traditions also assumed a community that was interpretive and interactive, not an audience of disciplined applauders. And in all such performances and festivals both ritual and subject matter reinvoked a despised colonial body and a voice that was anything but Anglo-ventriloquial—indeed was often subversive of such interpellation, treating it with deliberate irony. That West Indians long recognized and contrasted these two types of "oral" performance is attested across Caribbean cultures from nineteenth century Trinidad Carnival to contemporary works like Samuel Selvon's *The Housing Lark*, Erna Brodber's *Myal*, and Jamaica Kincaid's *Lucy*.

Two traditional characters of Trinidad Carnival over the last two centuries were "The English Pierrots" and "The Pierrots Grenades." As Al Creighton notes, these two characters (or groups of them) frequently engaged in contests that were both linguistic and physical. "The English Pierrot" was characterized by his recitation of

> stilted epics about great kings and battles and portions of English history, and . . . orations from Shakespeare, Julius Caesar, Mark Antony, Brutus, Othello, and excerpts from English and classical literature. He would also arm himself with questions on the literature and histories with which to battle his adversaries. (Creighton 61)

The English Pierrot is a "reciter," a reciter of English facts. The Pierrot Grenade, however, is a more complex character, one who has preserved a local skepticism in spite of some inescapable Anglo-interpellation. He thus makes fun of his own language and his Grenadian background "while lacing his performance with topical references and commentary, burlesque, badinage and satire" (Creighton 61). The performance of the English Pierrot is Anglo-ventriloquial, but the Pierrot Grenades (known as "the supreme jesters") did not study speeches and set-pieces, but used their wits on the spot in subversive encounters with their mirror-rivals. As Creighton notes, Pierrot Grenades usually appeared in groups of two to four, and the climax of their act was the spelling of words. This spelling is not a testing of conventional academic skill, as it might be for the English Pierrot (or as it was to be in appended questions to lessons in British-influenced school reading books) but is instead a "linking together of a series of verbal hieroglyphs in which words are spelt syllable by syllable, depending on puns and homonyms" (Creighton 61).

The carnival confrontation between the two kinds of Pierrots dramatized the ironies inherent in competing oral performances which on the one

hand re-produce and on the other traduce Anglo-imperialist scribal tradition. A version of this contest is "replayed" in Samuel Selvon's *The Housing
Lark* (1965) where Albert's response to Elouise's recitation invokes a traditional Caribbean mode while at the same time parodying English elocution.
Moreover Albert's response shifts the ground from voice to body as it
converts Elouise's stilted recitation pose into a part of his dance performance. Like the "English Pierrots" Elouise and her recitation become
incorporated within a Caribbean celebration subversive of an imperial
ventriloquial disembodiment:

> By the time the coach pull out from behind the market, like if
> fete start up right away. Fellars begin breaking bottle and spoon
> and singing calypso . . . and a mother encouraging her child
> "Go on Elouisa. Say that recitation that the English people
> teach you in school! Go on, don't play shy" and she turn to her
> neighbour and say "Just wait, she could really say poultry good,
> is only shy, she playing shy." The neighbour say "Albert not
> good at poultry, but if you see him twist! Albert? Where he
> gone to? Albert!?" And Elouisa stand up in the gangway biting
> her finger and swinging from side to side like how little girls do
> when they shy, and my boy Albert, as if he sense a partner,
> begin to twist in front of she. (108–9)

By incorporating (and thus satirizing) Anglo-recitation within alter/native
(and scribal) Caribbean performances, West Indians not only pointed to
the ironies of their own Anglo-interpellation, but reinvested the local with
authority over a ritual of obedience in which a Caribbean body, reproducing an Anglo-colonialist script, ventriloquised the imperial voice at the
colonial site.

Myal and Lucy are both concerned with the decolonizing of Anglo-
European fictions with resistance to recitation (in its broadest sense) and
the retrieval of the female Caribbean body from its imprisonment within
and hence erasure by European texts. Each traces a female protagonist's
progression from a moment of Anglo-recitation to a state of resistance and
potential recuperation.

The cryptic introductory chapter of *Myal* establishes the mysterious
illness of Ella O'Grady Langley, and the possibility of its cure with the aid
of the Afro-Jamaican skills of Mass Cyrus. But such a healing process will
prove lengthy, difficult and destructive. The seven days of *re*-creation
involve not just Mass Cyrus and Ella, but the entire Grove Town community, as well as the local flora and fauna. This first chapter thus encapsulates

the healing process of Myalism which will take Ella from the dis/ease of Anglo-interpellation recitation/reproduction, to the health of resistance and recuperation. The second chapter moves immediately to an episode emblematic of the contraction of the dis/ease Mass Cyrus is now called upon to cure—the child Ella's school recitation of Kipling's poem.

Although this recitation encapsulates one important aspect of inter-pellative education processes, the separation of mind from body that was an inevitable consequence of colonialist education is represented by the effect on Ella of the constant *reading* of texts from somewhere else. Her body (so often denigrated within those same texts) stays in Grove Town, Jamaica, but her mind moves elsewhere:

> When they brought out the maps and showed Europe, it rose from the paper in three dimensions, grew big, came right down to her seat and allowed her to walk on it, feel its snow, invited her to look deep down into its fiords and dykes . . . She met Peter Pan and she met the Dairy Maid . . .
> She had been to England several times. To Scotland too. . . . (11)

Ella has not actually been to Britain, but the passage neatly characterizes the imaginative inculcation of a colonial subjectivity which severs body from mind and invests "abroad," specifically the imperial centre, with the kind of reality/authority which imaginative, literary works most powerfully and profoundly evoke. The concomitant effect of this powerful re-production of England in Jamaica is of course the denigration of the local. Ella's body stays in Grove Town, but her mind, her imagination is (educated) elsewhere.

Brodber's metaphor for this process is "spirit thievery," and in *Myal* this takes a number of forms. Ella's "spirit" is thieved by colonialist educa-tion and reading practice, by a greater (imaginative) familiarity with and emotional investment in the world described in the books she reads. But it is also "thieved" in another way. The "raw materials" produced by colonies for the "mother country" did not simply consist in sugar, tobacco, minerals, oil. These "raw materials" also included character and narrative, new people and places to be "transported" to Europe and "captured" within Anglo-European representation. This aspect of "spirit thievery," closely allied to the "sick heart" psychology of Empire (i.e., the revivification of an old Europe through its exploitation of the "youth" of its colonies), is explored in the novel not through the European example, but as a more recent neocolonialist process.

Ella goes to the United States and there marries Selwyn Langley, a patent medicine magnate. Langley wishes to be a producer of stage shows, and seizes upon Ella's stories of her childhood in Grove Town. Thinking Ella will be pleased by his (grossly racist) representation of the "characters" of her Jamaican background, he produces a "coon show" and triumphantly presents it to his wife on opening night. The shock of this recognition of the "spirit thievery" of representation—a different form of the process of her earlier educational interpellation—precipitates the "blockage and swelling" Mass Cyrus is called upon to cure. But just as American patent medicine (or western medicine generally) could not help Ella's case, a full cure involves not only Mass Cyrus' healing wisdom, but a return to the *original* source of dis/ease, the schoolroom.

Ella becomes a school teacher and finds she is now part of the official process of reproduction of her own spirit thievery. With the help of Reverend Simpson, however, she evolves a strategy whereby her teaching skills may be deployed in the service of *de*colonisation not *re*colonisation. She can't refuse to teach the story of Mr Joe's farm since it is part of the syllabus, and since the children might read it anyway, but she can teach it differently. Instead of collusively reciting/reproducing its message of Empire loyalty and colonial obedience, she exposes its political purpose, teaching the text within the context of its *Jamaican* provenance, high-lighting its affective meaning within the crucially different contexts of its production and consumption. By refusing recitation and slavish reproduction, Ella teaches against the grain of "Mr Joe's Farm" reading for resistance and local restitution.

Myal also recounts the story of Mass Levi's terrorizing of Anita, a local manifestation of "spirit thievery" which is also healed by Myalism in the novel. But the Obeah practices of Mass Levi in Grove Town parallel the kind of "spirit thievery" anatomized in Ella's story. The loss of his sexual power provokes the once "upright" pillar of the community to attempt to regain his virility by absorbing the sexual potency of the teenage Anita. Mass Levi's mis-use of Obeah to revivify his old age again conjures the "sick heart" psychology of Empire—the attempt by the "old world" nations to enliven their cultures (and narratives) by "thieving" the spirits and bodies (and characters and plots) of their colonised subjects. And in its use of both Obeah and Myalism, Brodber's novel rejects the Western mind/body split at the same time as it traces the colonised's imprisonment within it. *Myal* thus demonstrates a rejection of the recitation of the Western text (in all its manifestations) and explores a technology of resti-tution and reclamation, a reintegration of mind and body.

Jamaica Kincaid's *Lucy* also traces a journey of retrieval of the body from recitation to resistance. Like Ella O'Grady, Lucy's "journey" from subjectified colonial ("poor visitor") to the rebel Lucy/ Lucifer "begins" with a moment of recitation—her perfect (if two-faced) performance of Wordsworth's "daffodil" poem.

Like Ella, Lucy comes to the United States from the Caribbean, from the island of Antigua, to look after the children of a wealthy white family. In *Lucy*, Wordsworth's poem read and/or performed at the colonial "periphery" becomes emblematic of the processes of conquest and coloni-sation, and of the ways in which that process interpellates a subjective in which the colonised become "brutes" and the colonisers are cast as the bringers of civilization, poetry and light. It is this particularly violent value-exchange which has made Lucy resentful of the recitation of Wordsworth's poem, though it is difficult for her to articulate the reasons. Talking to her new mistress, Mariah, about being made to "learn by heart a long poem about some flowers I would not see in real life until I was nineteen" (30), Lucy is sorry to disappoint Mariah's enthusiasm by casting "her beloved daffodils in a scene she had never considered, a scene of conquered and conquests; a scene of brutes masquerading as angels and angels portrayed as brute" (30), but

> how could I explain to her the feeling I had about daffodils—that it wasn't exactly daffodils, but that they would do as well as anything else? (29)

Daffodils in *Lucy* thus come to stand for this process of colonialist interpel-lation, and the novel details the progress of the protagonist from resentful but obedient reciter to the Lucy/Lucifer of the last pages who refuses to repeat her act of recitation in writing.

As a resentful reciter Lucy vows to forget the daffodils, and erase the hated poem from her memory. But she finds she can't. She is troubled by the flowers in dreams where she is chased down narrow streets and then smoth-ered by "bunches and bunches of those same daffodils" (18). Words pene-trate minds and bodies, and the scars left by "learning by heart" are not as easily disposed of as Mariah might hope, when, in spite of "the poem," she hopes Lucy will find the flowers lovely. To Mariah aesthetics and politics are easily separated; not so for Lucy. The flowers are "the size and shape of play teacups, or fairy skirts." Significantly, they look like "something to eat and something to wear at the same time," and though they appear beautiful and simple, they seem "as if made to erase a complicated and unnecessary idea" (29). Through Wordsworth's poem the politics of aesthetics has already been absorbed into Lucy's heart; she is dressed in it, but she has also eaten it, internalised, it. Consequently, where Mariah sees only "beautiful flowers," Lucy feels "sorrow and bitterness" (30). Lucy has difficulty explaining this to Mariah since "my heart and my thoughts were racing so that every time I tried to talk I stammered and by accident bit my own tongue" (29). Learning *by heart* the culture of others strangles self-expression—the absorption of their aesthetics, indeed their "tongue," cuts off one's own.

Four pervasive metaphors structure the novel: imprisonment (and punishment); daffodils and the colour yellow; tongues; and hearts. *Lucy* is divided into five sections: "Poor Visitor," "Mariah," "The Tongue," "Cold Heart," and "Lucy." Lucy thus moves from being named by someone else, according to *their* world (Mariah's husband Lewis terms her "poor visitor") to her true-true name "Lucy" (Lucifer) at the end. Although Mariah wishes to be Lucy's friend and confidant, she is actually Lucy's "master," a term Lucy uses as the real nature of the association is increasingly exposed. In the important section "The Tongue," the "poor visitor's" imprisonment within Massa's world begins to cease as Lucy hardens that once invaded heart against continuing capture within Euro-American ideas/texts/theories.

As Alison Donnell has noted, *Lucy* is a novel which interrogates and refuses Euro-American theories of many kinds, from those old fairy tales" of history, fiction, anthropology, to more contemporary notions of psychology and ecology. Lewis' and Mariah's interpretation of the world around them is constantly contrasted with that of Lucy, and their "axioms" are constantly relativised by her different views. The yellow of the daffodils (those flowers which "looked simple, as if made to erase a complicated and unnecessary idea") is associated throughout with the yellow of Mariah's hair and that of her clone-like children. It is a yellow substance "like cornmeal" which forms the ground on which Lewis chases her in her dream. The yellow of cornmeal conjures slave provisions and slavery and is associated with the colonialist "daffodil complex" Lucy strives to articulate to Mariah. But to Lewis and Mariah the significant aspect of the dream is the pit with the snakes. "Dr Freud for Visitor" Mariah archly remarks to Lewis, and both the stress on this particular aspect of the dream and the naturalization of a particular European interpretation of dreams exposes as culturally grounded *theories* which Lewis and Mariah regard as fact. Like the earlier "fixtures of fantasy" historically instilled in colonial subjects, these new "fixtures" are interrogated in *Lucy* by the different and often more complex interpretations offered by Lucy herself.

This "alternative" reading of a "classically Freudian" dream, emphasizing racial oppression over sexual psychology, does not of course deny the importance of gender oppression or the complex sexualities complicit in race oppression. But in *Lucy*, Lucy uses her sexuality against these oppressions, just as she uses the body to reclaim self-identity from the capture and abuse of the black female body within the European "book." If Lucy could not openly rebel against the recitation of Wordsworth in Antigua, in New York she increasingly rejects new European theories about her sexuality and her body offered by Mariah. She interrogates contemporary Euro-American feminism against the background of her own experience, wondering why Mariah relies on books to explain her life:

> This was something I knew, why didn't Mariah know it also? And if I were to tell it to her she would only show me a book she had somewhere which contradicted everything I said—a book most likely written by a woman who understood absolutely nothing. (141)

Mariah's simplicity and "innocence," her reliance on books, is contrasted early in the novel with another kind of body/script interaction. Relying on " theories" to explain her life, Mariah has little grasp of the way words enter and mark colonised bodies, and this is part of her "simplicity." Lucy understands the interpellative and body-marking (and body-erasing) power of text, but contrasts and counteracts its potential power with that of the body itself. Mariah's faith in her books is equated with her "yellow" simplicity, and her apparently perfect body is contrasted with that of Sylvie, Lucy's mother's friend who has been in jail. Sylvie has a mark like a rose on her face, a scar from a bite she received in a fight with another woman. This mark "bound her to something much deeper than its reality, something she could not put into words" (25). By contrast, Mariah "with her pale-yellow skin and yellow hair . . . looked blessed, no blemish or mark of any kind on her cheek or anywhere else" (27).

Sexuality becomes something powerfully experienced, not constructed within a European theoretical frame, and something through which women can themselves exercise a control over men's bodies, a control denied in sexual theories like Freud's. Lucy uses her "tongue" to manipulate male sexuality, never letting any of the boys she experiments with touch her "heart." In thinking of "all the other tongues I had held in my mouth" (82) Lucy associates sexuality, colonialism and recitation; and, resisting that fatal connection between "tongue" and "heart," she converts recitation to resistance. The two sections "The Tongue" and "Cold Heart" precede the final appearance of "Lucy" and the attainment of rebel angel status. By manipulating the tongues of others—putting *her* tongue in *their* mouths—Lucy takes back control of her own voice and body from capture

by European texts of all kinds, those persisting "fixtures of fantasy" (4) to
which Kincaid refers.

At the end of the novel Lucy takes out the notebook Mariah has given
her to begin writing her own text. But her first sentence indicates a persisting
enthrallment to written cliché. It is the body which comes to her rescue in
obliterating the re-production of the already-written:

> And then as I looked at this sentence a great wave of shame came
> over me and I wept so much that the tears fell on the page and
> caused all the words to become one great big blur. (164)

Lucy's body has erased a final act of scriptorial obedience.

HELEN PYNE TIMOTHY

Adolescent Rebellion and Gender Relations in
At the Bottom of the River *and* Annie John

Perhaps the most puzzling moments in Jamaica Kincaid's *At the Bottom of the River* and *Annie John* are those involving the emotional break between the mother and daughter and the violence of the daughter's response to her mother after that break. In the early stages of the narrative, Kincaid, chronicling the intense emotional bond in which they are wrapped, is at pains to detail the warmly affectionate upbringing Annie received from her mother. To the child the relationship was so satisfying that the father was almost shut out; in fact he operated on the periphery:

> As she told me the stories, I sometimes sat at her side, leaning against her, or I would crouch on my knees behind her back and lean over her shoulder. . . . At times I would no longer hear what it was she was saying: I just liked to look at her mouth as it opened and closed over words or as she laughed. How terrible it must be for all the people who had no one to love them so and no one whom they loved so, 1 thought. My father for instance. (*Annie John*, pp. 22–23)

Indeed, Kincaid creates such a perfect world of strongly nurturing mother figure and dependent child suffused with primary love that there can only

From *Caribbean Women Writers: Essays from the First International Conference*. © 1990 by Calaloux Publications.

be agreement when Annie says, "It was in such a paradise that I lived."

Nancy Chodorow, in her revealing study of psychoanalytic theory as it may be applied to the relationship of mother and daughter, has documented the pattern of absolute dependence in a primary love relationship that links the child to the nurturing mother figure. In the early years the mother is central to the focus of the child, idolized and idealized. Chodorow shows that the apprehension of the mother figure can be so strong that the child has to go through a period of rejection to separate subject/self from object/mother before development of the individual consciousness is possible. For the female child, this split comes at puberty and must, therefore, have important ramifications for the expression of her sexuality.

Annette Insanally has also illustrated the relevance of Jacques Lacan's theory of psychic development in her reading of *At the Bottom of the River* in commenting on "the mother/daughter figure in a strange inseparable love/hate syndrome where the father figure is tangential and indistinct but important." There can be no doubt that the findings of psychoanalytic theory form an important framing and structural device that shapes the particularities of the works and therefore strongly illuminates the workings of the inner life of the protagonist. All the elements of the classic stages of development of the girl from what Kincaid describes as a possible "life as predictable as an insect's and I am in my pupa stage . . . primitive and wingless" to the woman who must be confident in her own person, her selfhood, and her sexuality: "I shall grow to be a tall, graceful and altogether beautiful woman, and I shall impose on large numbers of people my will and also for my own amusement, great pain."

Both *At the Bottom of the River* and *Annie John* are primarily concerned with intense mother/daughter relationships, the psychic development of the girl child, the teaching and learning of appropriate gender roles, and the breaking of the strongly imposed image of the mother for the development of individuation in adulthood.

Obviously, these stages of psychic development take place within any culture, and presumably they provide evidence for a metatheory that has universal application. The concern of this essay is therefore to inquire whether, and in what ways, Kincaid has anchored the imaginative reworkings of these experiences within the particular culture of the Caribbean in such a way as indelibly to infuse the development of Annie and the nameless "girl" of *At the Bottom of the River* with a "local habitation and a name."

The stages of Annie's psychosocial development are all amplified within the context of Caribbean cultural practices and beliefs. In the early stage of intense primary love and involvement with the mother, the first hint of separation comes with the child's awareness of death and her understanding that the perceived integrated personality of the two might be split by the loss of one individual. Annie's perception of her mother begins to change when she realizes that her mother has links with a community outside of her own perception:

> One day, a girl smaller than I, a girl whose mother was a friend of my mother's, died in my mother's arms. I did not know this girl at all . . . I heard my mother describe to my father just how Nalda had died . . . My mother asked my father to make the coffin for Nalda, and he did, carving bunches of tiny flowers on the sides. Nalda's mother wept so much that my mother had to take care of everything and since children were never prepared by undertakers, my mother had to prepare the little girl to be buried. I then began to look at my mother's hands differently. They had stroked the dead girl's forehead, they had bathed and dressed her and laid her in the coffin my father had made. My mother would come back from the dead girl's house smelling of bay rum—a scent that for a long time afterward would make me feel ill. For a while, though not for very long, I could not bear to have my mother caress me or touch my food or help me with my bath. I especially couldn't bear the sight of her hands lying in her lap. (*Annie John*, pp. 56)

Here Annie's mother is closely involved in a momentous happening in which she was not the center. She could clearly envisage the possibility of her dying and leaving her mother as well as the possibility of her mother betraying the primary love tie and dying herself and leaving Annie, like her classmate, "such a shameful thing, a girl whose mother had died and left her alone in the world."

Furthermore, the details of the death rituals as delineated are strongly indicative of Caribbean cultural habits. Annie's mother must of necessity be available to her neighbor in times of sickness and death; she must assist in transporting the child to the doctor, must help with the laying out of the body, must support and nurture the mother through the time of grieving. The father assists by carving the handmade coffin. This act is his personal involvement, but the male figure is not central to the emotional ritual. Thus the death is reported to him by the mother; but it is she who is central to all its demands, and her involvement is personal. Of course, Annie's feelings toward death are ambivalent: she is deeply aware of the understanding that death could rob her of the most intensely loved person, her mother. Yet in her attempts at role-modeling she wishes to become schooled and to penetrate the secrets of the ritual so she can be like her mother, an important person in a gender-binding ritual.

The burgeoning perception of subject/self, object/mother reaches the moment of separation, as expected, at puberty. Annie begins to see everything about her mother in a negative light and, typically, transfers the intensity of her emotion to a friend, Gwen. Her sexual urges are beginning to develop, as is the awareness of her physical presence and that of others. What is interesting about the presentation here is the way the mother is portrayed as relating to her daughter's developments:

> The summer of the year I turned twelve, I could see that I had grown taller; most of my clothes no longer fit. . . . My legs had become spindle-like, the hair on my head even more unruly than usual, small tufts of hair had appeared under my arms and when I perspired the smell was strange, as if I had turned into a strange animal. I didn't say anything about it, and my mother and father didn't seem to notice, for they didn't say anything either. (*Annie John*, p. 25)

But in fact the parents had noticed, and the change in behavior manifested itself most violently in the mother, not the father. Kincaid seems to be making the statement here that in the Caribbean context, the mother is unable to continue successful role-modeling after the child reaches puberty. Up to this point, Annie's mother has been a strongly loving, caring, nurturing mother figure. Annie receives no beatings, only minor punishment. "I ate my supper outside, alone, under the breadfruit tree, and my mother said that she would not be kissing me goodnight later; but when I climbed into bed she came and kissed me anyway."

Moreover, Annie had been encouraged to model herself in every detail on her mother's conduct and behavior so as to become a perfect woman. Kincaid is at pains to show the mother's involvement with every detail of the child's development. The mementos of important stages in her prepubescent development are locked in a trunk to be taken out and lovingly recalled from time to time. But this Caribbean mother is unable to speak about the later stage of the child's development; she "didn't seem to notice." Kincaid's message seems to indict the Caribbean mother: she does not know how to communicate openly about the girl's development into a sexual being.

The contrast between the mother's attitudes in the girl's pre- and post-pubescent periods is almost shocking. In her relationship with Annie there had previously been a highly pleasurable integration of the child's body and the mother's as part of the relationship of loving and caring; and the child displayed an acutely sensitive response to her mother's body shape, touch, and smell. In this Caribbean family there is a lot of touching, hugging, and caressing between mother and daughter: the mother swims with the daughter on her back, they bathe together in an extended ritual which is firmly rooted in the bush-bath African-derived cultural habit where the body becomes almost a temple of good, but where the function and pleasure of sensation are not ruled out.

Up to puberty, then, the mother's role-modeling signals affirmatives about the body, sensation, and sensuality. These affirmatives are further reinforced in Annie's school life. Her friends in a girls' school, cut off from boys, are almost hysterical in their desire to "prove" their womanhood by growing breasts and menstruating. Annie's description of her first period is full of drama and emphasizes the emotions of awe and reverence, beauty even, in this event, and in the response of the other girls to whom it is revealed:

> At recess, among the tombstones, I of course had to exhibit and demonstrate. None of the others were menstruating yet. I showed everything without the least bit of flourish since my heart wasn't in it. I wished instead that one of the other girls were in my place and that I were just sitting there in amazement. How nice they all were, though, rallying to my side, offering shoulders on which to lean, laps in which to rest my weary, aching head, and kisses that really did soothe. (*Annie John*, p. 52)

Annie's personal response betrays the uncertainty of the moment engendered by the fear of the future which this watershed must of necessity entail. But the fear is devoid of any suggestion of shame or secrecy; rather, it is a fear of adulthood, of uncontrollable changes in her life.

The wild abandonment and pleasure in their physical personhood which the girls display is contrasted with the mother's attempts to suppress her own and Annie's after Annie entered puberty. What can be her motive, why does she deliberately cut herself off from the closeness of touch and caress, from wearing the same dresses, from accompanying her daughter on walks with her father? Is her desire to push Annie away into the perception of herself as other ("You just cannot go around the rest of your life looking like a little me") motivated by psychological primes, sexual jealousies, and uncertainties or social mores? Perhaps her actions arise out of a mixture of all these; but the discussion here will primarily consider the latter as part of a network of complex structures perceived by the child.

This child is an extraordinarily sensitive participant/observer of her mother's life; and at this stage her acuity is trained toward the asymmetrical aspects of her behavior which can now be negatively assessed. The most obvious and, for the child, the most confusing and searing are concerned with questions of sexuality between mother and father.

In *Annie John* the figure of the father is peripheral to the intense absorption that links the daughter to the mother. Nevertheless, to the pre-adolescent, he is an important love object. Interestingly enough, however, when Annie begins to assess her mother negatively, she also transfers her negative viewpoint to her father, who is then seen as being more a part of her mother's universe than of her own: "They were eating away as they talked, my father's false teeth making that clop-clop sound like a horse on a walk as he talked, my mother's mouth going up and down like a donkey's as she chewed each mouthful thirty-two times . . . I was looking at them with a smile on my face but disgust in my heart" (*Annie John*, p. 136). Even if there are adjustments for Annie's tendency to an overwrought sensibility in her emotional assessment of her parents, there is a suggestion of sexual jealousy in her perception of the mother's physical closeness to the father. Alexander's relations with other women, although they occurred before his marriage, also appear to have had some impact on Annie. Although this description that the father has had affairs and "outside children" which he does not acknowledge represents a social truth of Caribbean society, the fact that he has been intimate with women whom he now passes by without speaking in the street invests sensitive young Annie with a subliminal sense that there is something shameful in a sexual relationship. Kincaid seems to be indicating here that male sexuality has no consequences, whereas for females the consequences are severe.

But more important is the mother's ambivalence about her own sexuality; she has suppressed this aspect of herself in her role-modeling although she does at one point recommend marriage and motherhood to Annie. But these concepts seem divorced from any sexual involvement. Heterosexual involvement is seen by the child as sin and shame, not joy or pleasure.

It is therefore totally understandable that when Annie unexpectedly sees her mother joyfully engaged in a sexual act with her father she is thrown into an emotional turmoil that causes the split and antagonism of daughter and mother with its consequent consuming negative assessments of the mother's role and behavior. These negative assessments begin strongly with the inability of the mother to negotiate the meaning of the girl's burgeoning sexuality.

Indeed, the ambivalence of the Caribbean mother is reinforced by Annie's mother's extreme reaction to a most innocent meeting and greeting of three boys which Annie engages in on her way home from school. Kincaid describes:

On looking up, she observed me making a spectacle of myself in front of three boys. She went on to say that after all the years she had spent drumming into me the proper way to conduct myself when speaking to young men it had pained her to see me behave in the manner of a slut . . . in the street and that just to see me had caused her to feel shame. The word "slut" (in patois) was repeated over and over, until suddenly I felt as if I were drowning in a well but instead of the well being filled with water it was filled with the word "slut," and it was pouring in through my eyes, my ears, my nostrils, my mouth. As if to save myself I turned to her and said, "Well, like father like son, like mother like daughter." (*Annie John*, p. 102)

Of course, behind Annie's impudence lies the understanding that she has discovered a serious weakness in her erstwhile strong, dominant, and correct mother. Moreover, this weakness points to a deep-rooted ambivalence, an insecurity that brings into question the very basis of the mother's existence and can be read further as the mother's inability to transmit to her daughter a coherent value system that embraces the various aspects of her role as woman in a Caribbean society. Indeed, "Girl," in which the mother is the classic transmitter of culture and her function in the learning and teaching of the female role, overt within the context of the particular Caribbean society, demonstrates the uneasy mix between the two streams of Africa and Europe through which the mother has to thread her way and that of the child in her interpretations of the Creole world of the Caribbean.

Wash the white clothes on Monday and put them on the stone heap; wash the color clothes on Tuesday and put them on the clothesline to dry; don't walk bare-head in the hot sun; cook pumpkin fritters in very hot sweet oil, soak your little clothes right after you take them off, when buying cotton to make yourself a nice blouse . . . it is true that you sing benna in Sunday school? always eat your food in such a way that it won't turn someone else's stomach; on Sundays try to walk like a lady and not like the slut you are so bent on becoming; don't sing benna in Sunday school; you must'nt speak to *wharf-rat boys, not even to give directions* . . . this is how to hem a dress when you see the hem coming down and so to prevent yourself from looking *like the slut I know you are so bent on becoming* . . . this is how you sweep a corner; this is how you sweep a whole house; t*his is how you sweep a yard*; this is how you smile to someone you don't like too much;

this is how you smile to someone you don't like at all; this is how
you smile to someone you like completely; this is how you set a
table for tea; this is how you set a table for dinner. . . this is how
you set a table for breakfast; this is how to behave in the presence
of men who don't know you very well, and this way they won't
recognize immediately the slut I have warned you against
becoming; be sure to wash every day, even if it is with your own
spit; don't squat down to play marbles—you are not a boy, you
know; don't pick people's flowers—you might catch something;
don't throw stones at blackbirds, because it might not be a blackbird at all. . . . This is how to make a good medicine for a cold;
this is how to make a good medicine to throw away a child before
it even becomes a child; this is how to catch a fish; this is how to
throw back a fish you don't like, and that way something bad
won't fall on you; this is how to bully a man; this is how a man
bullies you; this is how to love a man, and if this doesn't work
there are other ways, and if they don't work don't feel too bad
about giving up. (*At the Bottom of the River*, pp. 3–5)

This quasi-monologue of the mother with the occasional indignant
interjections of the daughter is strongly revelatory of the ambivalences that
invest the role-modeling of the Caribbean mother, particularly since she
herself has serious conflicts. As we have already seen, sexuality is almost
instantly related to sluttishness, possibly because of the mother's fear that her
daughter will become the exploited female of "wharf-rat boys" or even of the
father's former lovers, who view her with hate, in other words, will lose her
chance to rise in class, in the world. There is also the possibility that, with
the male who is acceptable in class, sexuality is possible, even desirable: "this
is how to love a man, and if this doesn't work there are other ways." The girl
is being urged to use her womanly wiles to accomplish results from an act she
is simultaneously being taught is shameful. Included here is also a recognition that a woman's sexuality must be used to accomplish a rise in social
status—possibly an unconscious explanation for the beautiful, strong, young
mother's marriage to a much older, weaker, far less beautiful husband, who
offered her marriage and a comfortable home.

Moreover, the Caribbean mother who is bent on seeing her daughter
rise from the lower classes to the middle ranks must not only teach her useful
housekeeping tasks, cleanliness, good manners, and practical knowledge of
her environment but also European norms and the need to desist in the practice of African ones. The girl perceives these paradoxes inherent in the
mother's relationship to her own Caribbean culture, and they become part of

the negative features that help reinforce the split between the egos of mother and daughter and the daughter's subsequent rebellion. Thus in the mother's perception, Christianity, Sunday school, good manners (the ability to curtsy), and piano lessons are all essential to her daughter's acceptability and respectability. Consequently she must not sing benna (folk/African songs) in Sunday school; but Christian training becomes far less important when dealing with the real problems of life. Here the mother falls back on the belief in folk wisdom, myth, African systems of healing and bush medicine, the mysteries of good and evil spirits inhabiting the perceived world of nature. "Don't pick people's flowers—you might catch something; don't throw stones at blackbirds, because it might not be a blackbird at all. . . . This is how to make a good medicine for a cold; this is how to throw away a child before it even becomes a child."

It is therefore significant that Kincaid juxtaposes the event that causes Annie's awakening to this dimension of her mother's life with her return from Sunday school. For the child there is a complicated clash of eschatological systems which she cannot articulate. She can only feel that some important principle has been violated which she attributes to her mother's hypocrisy.

Annie's rebellions are directed primarily against her mother's notions of respectability—being "a lady" in her sense of what would be required for the socially ambitious in a European context: the battle of wills takes place over Annie's lessons in good manners ("how to meet and greet important people in the world"), piano lessons, Christianity, and a good European-style secondary education. The emotional split leads to a clash and finally an isolation of Annie that becomes so burdensome it leads to a mental breakdown.

The signals given during this period of mental and emotional collapse confirm the insecurity of the search for a coherent cosmology in which the child's social ambition, her intellectual and romantic yearnings, gleaned from European books (Blyton, the Brontes) and a European education, her moral, spiritual, and cultural landscape, and her sexual urges can all be accommodated.

Such complexities can never be completely resolved, but Kincaid is careful to guide the reader. There is the obvious sexual symbolization of the washing of the photographs (all of the people in white) of herself at her First Communion, her Aunt Mary at her wedding, and her father in cricket gear (white) "to remove the dirt from the front of my father's trousers." Next, the episode with Mr. Nigel is instructive. Mr. Nigel, his fishing partner, and Miss Catherine, the woman they share harmoniously, are firmly anchored in a world free of pretensions or intrusion from any imported system of value. Their untrammeled security provides a wholeness, a kind of truth for which Annie longs.

But the most important influence on Annie at this time is the formidable figure of Ma Chess, the grandmother. Kincaid has cast her in a fully African world. She inhabits the world of the African spirits and, as long as she remains true to that vision, is able to control life and death. Her beloved son dies when she defers to the unbelief of Pa Chess and gets a doctor about an illness which "the doctor knew nothing about, and the obeah woman knew everything about." After that irretrievable and distressing error her commitment to the African-Caribbean spiritual universe is total and unwavering. In her Kincaid has provided a portmanteau figure of African myth and reality: Ma Chess is African healer, bush medicine specialist, and Caribbean obeah woman, extremely conscious of the presence of good and evil in life and able to ward off evil. She is also the mythological "flying African" able to cross the seas without a boat, and the flying "soucouyant" (female witch) who lives in a hole in the ground. Her world, however, is not threatening to the child but comforting and healing because of its coherency, its validity, and its verity. As Annie describes the healing relationship,

> Ma Chess is on the floor at the foot of my bed, eating and sleeping there, and soon I grew to count on her smells and the sound her breath made as it went in and out of her body. Sometimes at night, when I would feel that I was all locked up in the warm falling soot and could not find my way out Ma Chess would come into my bed with me and stay until I was myself— ... I would lie on my side curled up like a little comma, and Ma Chess would be next to me, curled up like a bigger comma, into which I fit. (*Annie John*, p. 126)

This tension-free relationship is typical of a grandmother/granddaughter link, but it also records the sense of security the conforming world of Ma Chess exudes. A valid sociological point emerges here: for some of the older generation of Caribbean women, the penetration of European cultural values into the African cosmology was not so intense or so desirable. Most of these systems of belief, syncretism, are beginning to appear in Annie's mother's universe. Annie herself is going to "somewhere; Belgium," the heart of Europe, far away and in rejection of "obeah women" (African systems of belief). But there is a recognition that like her grandmother and mother before her, she must carry a trunk, that is, the cultural baggage of a race, a country, and a class, although for each generation, the trunks are packed with different contents.

What a complex moral cosmology Caribbean girls must inhabit and how ambivalent are the signals passed on to them. But even in the act of rebellion Kincaid strongly shows that the break between mothers and daughters can never be final or complete, that the women are linked irrevocably to each other by ties that are finally inextricable.

Chronology

1949   Born Elaine Potter Richardson, May 25, Holberton Hospital, St. John's, Antigua.
Her mother, Annie Richardson Drew, was born in Dominica, and is a homemaker and political activist.

> (Mother's family, surname Richardson, were land peasants in Dominica; maternal grandmother, Carib Indian; grandfather's occupation: policeman.)

Biological father, Frederick Potter, who does not play a significant role in her childhood, was a former taxi driver, now is employed at the Mill Reef Club in Antigua.
Stepfather and the man she knows as her father, David Drew, is a cabinetmaker and carpenter.

1952   Mother teaches her to read and enrolls her in the Moravian School at age three.

1956   Attends the Antiguan Girls School.
Apprenticed to a seamstress.
Attends Princess Margaret School.

1958   Joseph Drew, her first brother, is born.

1959   Dalma Drew, her second brother, is born.

1961   Devon Drew, her third brother, is born.

1965-1973 Elaine Potter Richardson leaves Antigua for the United States
              shortly after her sixteenth birthday.
              Works as an au pair in Scarsdale, N.Y., then as a receptionist and
              as a magazine writer for *Art Direction*.
              Takes classes at Westchester Community College in White Plains.
              Works as an au pair on the Upper East Side.
              File Clerk and secretary at Magnum Photos.
              Obtains high school diploma.
              Studies photography at the New York School for Social Research.
              Attends Franconia College in New Hampshire.

1973   Changes name to Jamaica Kincaid.
              First publication, the short story *When I Was Seventeen*.
              Works as a freelance writer for *Ms., Ingenue, Village Voice*.

1976   *New Yorker* staff writer, where her gardening column appears
              regularly.

1979   Marries Allen Shaw, a composer and teacher at Bennington
              College.

1983   Receives an American Academy and Institute of Arts and Letters
              Prize for *At the Bottom of the River*.

1984   Receives the Morton Dauwen Zabel Award for fiction.

1985   Annie, her daughter, is born.
              Moves to Vermont.
              Finalist for Ritz Paris Hemmingway Award.
              Returns for a visit to Antigua; informally banned from the island.

1989   Recipient of a Guggenheim fellowship.
              Harold, her son, is born.

1991   Receives honorary degrees from Williams College and Long
              Island College.

1992   Informal ban on visiting Antigua apparently lifted.

1996   Resigns as *New Yorker* staff writer, citing creative differences with new editor, Tina Brown.

1997   Receives a PEN/Faulkner Award.

Contributors

HAROLD BLOOM is Sterling Professor of Humanities at Yale University and Professor of English at New York University. He is the author of *The Visionary Company*, *The Anxiety of Influence*, *Poetry and Repression*, and other volumes of literary criticism. His forthcoming study, *Freud, Transference and Authority*, considers all of Freud's major writings. A MacArthur Prize Fellow, Professor Bloom is general editor of five series of literary criticism published by Chelsea House.

GIOVANNA COVI has a degree in Anglo-American literature from the University of Venice, Italy. A recent graduate of the Ph.D. program in English at SUNY-Binghamton, her dissertation is titled "The Slow Process of Decolonializing Language: The Politics and Sexual Difference in Post-modernist Fictions."

LAURA NIESEN DE ABRUNA is an associate professor of English at Ithaca College, N.Y. Her work focuses on Anglophone Caribbean women writers and has appeared in *Modern Fiction Studies* and *World Literature Written in English*.

ALISON DONNELL lectures in Post-Colonial literatures at the University of Leeds, England. Her doctoral thesis examined Jamaican women's poetry from 1900–1945. She has also coedited (with Sarah Lawrence Welsh) *The Routledge Reader in Caribbean Literature* (1996).

MOIRA FERGUSON holds the James E. Ryan Chair in English and Women's Literature at the University of Nebraska. Her books include *Subject to Others: British Women Writers 1578-1799* (1985), *Colonialism and Gender Relations from Mary Wollstonecraft to Jamaica Kincaid: East Caribbean Connections* (1993), and *Jamaica Kincaid: Where Land Meets Body* (1994).

PATRICIA ISMOND, a senior lecturer in the Department of English at the St. Augustine Campus of the University of the West Indies in Trinidad, is from St. Lucia in the West Indies. Having done extensive work on Derek Walcott, her books include *Self-Portrait of an Island: St. Lucia through the Eyes of its Writers* (1986) and *Walcott vs. Brathwaite* (1993).

SUSAN SNIADER LANSER is a professor of Comparative Literature, Women's Studies, and English at the University of Maryland, where she directs the Comparative Literature Program. Her books include *The Narrative Act: Point of View in Prose Fiction* (1981) and *Fictions of Authority: Women Writers and Narrative Voice* (1992).

H. ADLAI MURDOCH is an assistant professor of French and Francophone Literature at the University of Illinois. His work, which has appeared in *entralogos*, *Callaloo*, *Research in African Literatures*, and *Yale French Studies*, examines the intersections of postcolonial discourse and narrative theory, with particular reference to the French Caribbean.

EDYTA OCZKOWICZ, educated in Poland and England, is an assistant professor of English at Salem College. Her areas of special interest include twentieth century ethnic and immigrant women writers in America.

DONNA PERRY is an assistant professor of English at William Patterson College, N.J., where she teaches literature and women's studies courses. She is the author of *Backtalk: Women Writers Speak Out, Interviews* (1993) and has co-edited (with Nan Bauer Magliu) *"Bad Girls"/Good Girls": Women, Sex, and Power in the Nineties* (1996).

HELEN TIFFIN is a professor of English at the University of Queensland, Australia. She is the author (with Bill Ashcroft and Gareth Griffiths) of *The Empire Writes Back* (1989) and has written articles on post-colonial literatures and literary theory. She has also co-edited (with Ian Adam) *Past the Last Post* (1990) and (with Ashcroft and Griffiths) *The Post-Colonial Reader* (1995).

HELEN PYNE TIMOTHY, formerly dean of the Faculty of Arts and General Studies and head of the Department of Language and Linguistics at the University of the West Indies, was a visiting assistant professor at the Africana Studies and Research Center, Cornell University, during the spring of 1994. Her interests include African American and Caribbean literature, Creole linguistic theory, and women's writing from Africa and the Diaspora.

Bibliography

Covi, Giovanna. *Out of the Kumbla: Caribbean Women and Literature*. Trenton, N.J.: Africa World Press, 1990.

Cudjoe, Selwyn R., ed. *Caribbean Women Writers: Essays from the First International Conference*. Wellesley, Mass.: Calaloux Publications, 1990.

Donnell, Alison. "She Ties Her Tongue: The Problems of Cultural Paralysis in Post-colonial Criticism." *ARIEL*, January 1995: 101–16.

Ferguson, Moira. "*Lucy* and the Mark of the Colonizer." *Modern Fiction Studies*, Summer 1993: 237–56.

Higonnet, Margaret. *Borderwork*. Ithaca, N.Y.: Cornell University Press, 1994.

Ismond, Patricia. "Jamaica Kincaid: First They Must Be Children." *World Literature Written in English*. Autumn 1988: 336–40.

Murdoch, H. Adlai. "Severing the (M)Other Connection: The Representation of Cultural Identity in Jamaica Kincaid's *Annie John*." *Callaloo* 13:2 (Spring 1990): 325–40.

Nasta, Susheila, ed. *Motherlands: Black Women's Writing from Africa, the Caribbean, and South Asia*. London: The Women's Press Limited, 1991.

Oczkowicz, Edyta. "Jamaica Kincaid's *Lucy*: Cultural "Translation" as a Case of Creative Exploration of the Past." *MELUS*, Fall 1996: 143–56.

Tiffin, Helen. "Cold Hearts and (Foreign) Tongues: Recitation and the Reclamation of the Female Body in the Works of Erna Brodber and Jamaica Kincaid." *Callaloo* 16:4 (Fall 1993): 909–21.

Acknowledgements

"Jamaica Kincaid and the Resistance to Canons" by Giovanna Covi from *Out of the Kumbla: Caribbean Women and Literature*, copyright 1990 by Africa World Press. Reprinted by permission.

"Family Connections: Mother and Mother Country in the Fiction of Jean Rhys and Jamaica Kincaid" by Laura Niesen de Abruna, copyright 1991 by Laura Niesen de Abruna. Reprinted by permission.

"She Ties Her Tongue: The Problems of Cultural Paralysis in Postcolonial Criticism" by Alison Donnell from *ARIEL* (January 1995), copyright 1992 by Alison Donnell. Reprinted by permission.

"*Lucy* and the Mark of the Colonizer" by Moira Ferguson from *Modern Fiction Studies* (Summer 1993), copyright 1993 by Moira Ferguson. Reprinted by permission.

"Jamaica Kincaid: First They Must Be Children" by Patricia Ismond from *World Literature Written in English* (Autumn 1988), copyright 1988 by Patricia Ismond. Reprinted by permission.

"Compared to What? Global Feminism, Comparatism, and the Master's Tools" by Susan Sniader Lanser from *Borderwork*, edited by Margaret R. Higonnet, copyright 1994 by Cornell University Press. Reprinted by permission.

"Severing the (M)Other Connection: The Representation of Cultural Identity in Jamaica Kincaid's *Annie John*" by H. Adlai Murdoch from *Callaloo* 13:2 (Spring 1990), copyright 1990 by The Johns Hopkins University Press. Reprinted by permission.

"Jamaica Kincaid's *Lucy*: Cultural 'Translation' as a Case of Creative Exploration of the Past" by Edyta Oczkowicz from *MELUS* (Fall 1996), copyright 1996 by *MELUS*. Reprinted by permission.

"Initiation in Jamaica Kincaid's *Annie John*" by Donna Perry from *Caribbean Women Writers: Essays from the First International Conference*, edited by Selwyn R. Cudjoe, copyright 1990 by Calaloux Publications. Reprinted by permission.

"Cold Hearts and (Foreign) Tongues: Recitation and the Reclamation of the Female Body in the Works of Erna Brodber and Jamaica Kincaid" by Helen Tiffin from *Callaloo* 16:4 (Fall 1993), copyright 1993 by The Johns Hopkins University Press. Reprinted by permission.

"Adolescent Rebellion and Gender Relations in *At the Bottom of the River* and *Annie John*" by Helen Pyne Timothy from *Caribbean Women Writers: Essays from the First International Conference*, edited by Selwyn R. Cudjoe, copyright 1990 by Calaloux Publications. Reprinted by permission.

Index